VENUS

A Play by SUZAN-LORI PARKS

Theatre Communications Group

Venus is published by Theatre Communications Group, Inc., 520 Eighth Avenue, 24th Floor, New York, NY 10018–4156.

Page x: "Le travail humain," Jean-Luc Godard, the film *Masculin*Feminin*, 1966, Argos Films. "You don't believe in history," Virginia Woolf, *Between the Acts*, © 1941 by Virginia Woolf, Harcourt Brace, Jovanovich, New York.

This publication is made possible in part with public funds from the New York State Council on the Arts, a State Agency.

TCG books are exclusively distributed to the book trade by Consortium Book Sales and Distribution.

Parks, Suzan-Lori.
Venus / Suzan-Lori Parks.
ISBN-13: 978-1-55936-135-4
ISBN-10: 1-55936-135-2
I. Title.
PS3566.A736V46   1997
8129 .54—dc21   97–5739
    CIP

Cover design by Paula Scher
Text design and composition by Lisa Govan

First Edition, September 1997
Ninth Printing, November 2019

VENUS

with Love from **The Rockefeller Foundation's Bellagio**
with Love from **TCG**

and with Love from **Liz Diamond**
and with Love from **Thalia Field**
and with Love from **Bonnie Metzgar**
and with Love from **Bruce Hainley**
and with Love from **Stephanie Ellen**
and with Love from **David Harris**
and with Love from **Saartjie Baartman**

Production History

Venus was co-commissioned by The Women's Project and Pro-
ductions, Inc., New York City, Julia Miles, Artistic Director;
and Life on the Water, San Francisco, Susan Sillans, Bill Talen,
Artistic Directors. It was originally produced by the Joseph
Papp Public Theater/New York Shakespeare Festival, George C.
Wolfe, Producer; and Yale Repertory Theatre, Stan Wojewodski,
Jr., Artistic Director. It was first performed on March 28, 1996
at Yale Repertory Theatre. Scenic design was by Richard
Foreman, costume design by Paul Tazewell, lighting design by
Heather Carson and original music by Phillip Johnston.
Richard Foreman directed the following cast:

Miss Saartjie Baartman/The Girl/
  The Venus Hottentot . . . . Adina Porter
The Man/The Baron Docteur . . . . Peter Francis James
The Mans Brother/The Mother-Showman/
  The Grade-School Chum . . . . Sandra Shipley
The Negro Resurrectionist . . . . Mel Johnson, Jr.

The Chorus:

Cedric Harris   Adriane Lenox
Lynn Hawley   Thomas Jay Ryan
Kevin Isola   Ben Shenkman
John Lathan   Rainn Wilson

The Roles

- Miss Saartjie Baartman, a.k.a. The Girl, and later
  The Venus Hottentot
- The Man, later The Baron Docteur
- The Mans Brother, later The Mother-Showman, later
  The Grade-School Chum
- The Negro Resurrectionist
- The Chorus *as*:

    The Chorus of the 8 Human Wonders
    The Chorus of the Spectators
    The Chorus of the Court
    The Chorus of the 8 Anatomists
    The Players of *"For the Love of the Venus"*

Within *Venus* are scenes from *"For the Love of the Venus,"*
a Drama in 3 Acts.

The Characters:

The roles should be cast from The Chorus.

- The Father
- The Mother
- The Young Man

- The Uncle
- The Bride-to-Be (later, guised
  as "The Hottentot Venus")

List of Scenes

Author's Notes: From *"The Elements of Style"*

In *Venus* I'm continuing the use of my slightly unconventional theatrical elements. Here's a road map.

- *(Rest)*
  Take a little time, a pause, a breather; make a transition.

- A Spell
  An elongated and heightened *(Rest)*. Denoted by repetition of figures' names with no dialogue. Has sort of an architectural look:

The Venus
The Baron Docteur
The Venus
The Baron Docteur

This is a place where the figures experience their pure true simple state. While no action or stage business is necessary, directors should fill this moment as they best see fit.

- [Brackets in the text indicate optional cuts for production.]

- (Parentheses around dialogue indicate softly spoken passages (asides; sotto voce).)

Le travail humain
Ressucite les choses
D'entre les mortes.

> **—Jean-Luc Godard**
> *Masculin*Feminin*

"You don't believe in history,"
said William.

> **—Virginia Woolf**
> *Between the Acts*

Overture

The Venus facing stage right. She revolves, counterclockwise. 270 degrees. She faces upstage.

The Negro Resurrectionist
The Venus Hottentot!

The Mans Brother, later The Mother-Showman, later The Grade-School Chum
The Venus Hottentot!

The Man, later The Baron Docteur
The Venus Hottentot!
(Rest)   The Venus revolves 90 degrees. She
(Rest)   faces stage right.

The Chorus
The Chorus of the 8 Human Wonders!

The Man, later The Baron Docteur
The Man, later
The Baron Docteur!

The Negro Resurrectionist
The Negro Resurrectionist!

The Mans Brother, later The Mother-Showman, later The Grade-School Chum
The Brother, later
The Mother-Showman! Later
The Grade-School Chum

The Negro Resurrectionist

The Negro Resurrectionist!

The Chorus

The Chorus of the 8 Anatomists!
(Rest)   The Venus revolves 180 degrees.
(Rest)   She faces stage left.

The Man, later The Baron Docteur

The Chorus of the 8 Anatomists!

The Negro Resurrectionist

The Man, later
The Baron Docteur!

The Man, later The Baron Docteur

The Negro Resurrectionist!

The Mans Brother, later The Mother-Showman, later The Grade-School Chum

The Chorus of the Spectators!

The Negro Resurrectionist and The Man, later The Baron Docteur

The Brother, later
The Mother-Showman! Later
The Grade-School Chum!

The Man and The Mans Brother

The Negro Resurrectionist!

The Mans Brother, later The Mother-Showman, later The Grade-School Chum

The Chorus of the Court!

All

The Venus Hottentot!
(Rest)

The Venus

The Venus Hottentot.
(Rest)
(Rest)

The Negro Resurrectionist
I regret to inform you that thuh Venus Hottentot iz dead.

All
Dead?

The Mans Brother, later The Mother-Showman, later The Grade-School Chum
There wont b inny show tonite.

The Chorus
Dead!

The Negro Resurrectionist
Exposure iz what killed her, nothin on
and our cold weather. 23 days in a row it rained.
Thuh doctor says she drank too much. It was thuh cold I think.

The Man, later The Baron Docteur
Dead?

The Negro Resurrectionist
Deh-duh.

The Mans Brother, later The Mother-Showman, later The Grade-School Chum
I regret to inform you that the Venus Hottentot iz dead.
There wont b inny show tonite.

The Negro Resurrectionist
Diggidy-diggidy-diggidy-diggidy.

The Mans Brother, later The Mother-Showman, later The Grade-School Chum
Im sure yr disappointed.
We hate to let you down.
But 23 days in a row it rained.

The Negro Resurrectionist
Diggidy-diggidy-diggidy-dawg.

The Man, later The Baron Docteur
I say:
Perhaps,
she died of drink.

The Negro Resurrectionist
It was thuh cold I think.

The Venus
Uhhhh!

The Chorus
Turn uhway. Dont look. Cover her face. Cover yr eyes.

The Venus
Uhhhh!

[The Chorus
(Drum. Drum. Drum. Drum.)
(Drum. Drum. Drum. Drum.)

A Chorus Member
They came miles and miles and miles and miles and miles.
Comin in from all over to get themselves uh look-see.
They heard the drum.

The Mans Brother, later The Mother-Showman, later The Grade-School Chum
Drum. Drum.

The Chorus
(Drum. Drum.)**]**

The Mans Brother/Mother-Showman/Chum	**The Chorus**
DRUM	(drum)
DRUM	(drum)
DRUM	(drum)
DRUM.	(drum.)

The Venus
(I regret to inform you that thuh Venus Hottentot iz dead.
There wont b inny show tuhnite.)

The Chorus
(Outrage! Its an outrage!)

The Man, later The Baron Docteur
Dead?

The Negro Resurrectionist
Deh-duh.

The Mans Brother, later The Mother-Showman, later The Grade-School Chum
Tail end of r tale for there must be an end
is that Venus, Black Goddess, was shameles, she sinned or else
completely unknowing of r godfearin ways she stood
totally naked in her iron cage.

The Chorus
Shes thuh main attraction she iz
loves thuh sideshows center ring.
Whats thuh show without thuh star?

The Venus
Hum Drum Hum Drum.

The Chorus
Outrage! Its an outrage!
Gimmie gimmie back my buck!

The Mans Brother, later The Mother-Showman, later The Grade-School Chum
Behind that curtain just yesterday awaited:
Wild Female Jungle Creature. Of singular anatomy. Physiqued
in such a backward rounded way that she outshapes
all others. Behind this curtain just yesterday alive uhwaits
a female—creature
an out—of towner
whos all undressed awaiting you
to take yr peek. So youve heard.

All
We've come tuh see your Venus.

The Man and The Mans Brother
We know youre disuhpointed.
We hate tuh let you down.

The Negro Resurrectionist
A scene of Love:

The Venus
Kiss me
Kiss me
Kiss me *Kiss*

[The Man, later The Baron Docteur
I look at you, V
and I see Love

The Venus
Uhhhhhh!
Uhhhhhh!

The Chorus
Turn uhway. Dont look. Cover yr face. Cover yr eyes.

The Mans Brother, later The Mother-Showman, later The Grade-School Chum
She gained fortune and fame by not wearing a scrap
hiding only the privates that lipped in her lap.

The Chorus and The Man, later The Baron Docteur
Good God. Golly. Lookie-Lookie-Look-at-her.
Ooh-la-la. What-a-find. Hubba-hubba-hubba.

A Chorus Member
They say that if I pay uh little more
I'll get tuh look uh little longer
and for uh little more on top uh that
I'll get tuh stand
stand off tuh thuh side
in thuh special looking place.

A Chorus Member
(And from there if Im really quick I'll stick
my hand inside her
cage and have a feel
(if no ones looking).)

All
Hubba-hubba-hubba-hubba.

The Venus
Hum Drum Hum Drum.]

All
THE VENUS HOTTENTOT
THE ONLY LIVING CREATURE OF HER KIND IN THE
    WORLD
AND ONLY ONE STEP UHWAY FROM YOU RIGHT NOW
COME SEE THE HOT MISS HOTTENTOT
STEP IN STEP IN.

The Venus
Hur-ry! Hur-ry!

All
Hur-ry! Hur-ry!

The Venus
But I regret to inform you that thuh Venus Hottentot iz dead.
There wont b inny show tuhnite.

All
Outrage Its an outrage!
Gimmie Gimmie back my buck!

The Negro Resurrectionist
Hear ye Hear ye Order Order!

All
The Venus Hottentot iz dead.

The Negro Resurrectionist
All rise.

A Chorus Member
Thuh gals got bottoms like hot air balloons.
Bottoms and bottoms and bottoms pilin up like
like 2 mountains. Magnificent. And endless.
An ass to write home about.
Well worth the admission price.
A spectacle a debacle a priceless prize, thuh filthy slut.

Coco candy colored and dressed all in *au naturel*
she likes when people peek and poke.

The Venus
Hum drum hum drum.

The Mans Brother, later The Mother-Showman, later The Grade-School Chum
Step in step in step in step in.

The Venus
There wont b inny show tuhnite.

The Man, later The Baron Docteur and The Chorus
Hubba-hubba-hubba-hubba.

The Venus
She gained fortune and fame by not wearin uh scrap
hidin only thuh privates that lipped inner lap.

A Chorus Member
I look at you, Venus, and see:
Science. You
in uh pickle
on my library shelf.

The Venus
Uhhhhhh!
Uhhhhhh!
Uhhhhhh!
Uhhhhhh!

All
Order Order Order Order!
(Rest)

The Negro Resurrectionist
Tail end of our tale for there must be an end
is that Venus, Black Goddess, was shameles, she sinned or else
completely unknowing of r godfearin ways she stood
totally naked in her iron cage.
She gaind fortune and fame by not wearin a scrap

hidin only the privates lippin down from her lap.
When Death met her Death deathd her and left her to rot
au naturel end for our hot Hottentot.
And rot yes she would have right down to the bone
had not The Docteur put her corpse in his home.
Sheed a soul which iz mounted on Satans warm wall
while her flesh has been pickled in Sciences Hall.

Curtain. Applause.

*Scene 31: May I Present to You "The African Dancing
Princess"/She'd Make a Splendid Freak*

> Southern Africa, early 1800s. The Girl on hands and knees
> with scrub brush and bucket scrubs a vast tile floor.
> She is meticulous and vigorous. The floor shines.
> The Man and his Brother walk about. They are deep in conversation.

The Brother
So yll finance me?
Yes or No.

The Man
Last time you wanted money lets see what wuz it.
Damn, it slips my mind nope Ive got it now:
A Menagerie:
"Gods Entire Kingdom All Under One Roof."
A miserable failure.

The Brother
I didnt know theyd die in captivity.

The Man
Should of figured on that, Brother.

The Brother
I fed and watered them.

The Man
An animal needs more than that but God
you never were a farmer.

The Brother
Never was never will be.
(Rest)

Girl, you missed a spot.
(Rest)

The Negro Resurrectionist
Scene 31:
May I Present to You "The African Dancing Princess"/
She'd Make a Splendid Freak.
(Rest)

The Brother
So yll finance me? Yes or No.

The Man
I need to think on it.

The Brother
Whats there to think on?
A simple 2 year investment. Back me
and I'll double yr money no lets think big:
I'll triple it.

The Man
You need a girl. Wholl go all that way to be a dancer?

The Brother
Finding the girls the easy part.
(Rest)
That girl for instance.
Shes good. Vigorous and meticulous.

The Man
(You dont know her?)

The Brother
Cant say I do.
Yll back me, Man? Say yes.

The Man
Scheme #3 remember?
You went to Timbuktu.

The Brother
What of it.

The Man
Timbuktu to collect wild flowers?
Wild flowers to bring back here.
"Garden Exotica" admission 2 cents.

The Brother
They didnt take. Our soils too rich.

The Man
I lost my shirt!

The Brother
And like a lizard anothers grown back in its place. Back me!
This time Ive got a sure thing.
Ive done tons of background research. This schemell bite!

The Man
A "Dancing African Princess?"

The Brother
The English like that sort of thing.

The Man
(You really dont remember that girl?)

The Brother
Not from this angle.
(Rest)
Theres a street over there lined with Freak Acts
but not many dark ones, thats how we'll cash in.

The Man
A "Dancing African Princess."

The Brother
Im begging on my knees!

The Man
Get up. Youve got it.

The Brother
Just like a brother!

The Man
I am yr brother.

The Man and The Brother
Heh heh. Heh heh.

The Man
(You really dont remember her?)

The Brother
Enlighten me.

The Man
(Scheme #1?)

The Brother
(Marriage with the Hottentot—thats her?)

The Man
Father recognized the joke straight off
but Mother poor thing she still gives you funny looks.
You were barely 12.

The Brother
Shes grown.

The Man
As they all do.
Big Bottomed Girls. Thats their breed.
You were at one time very into it.

The Brother
Big Bottomed Girl. A novelty.
Shes vigorous and meticulous.
(Watch this, Brother!)
(Oh, whats her name?)

The Man
Her—? Saartjie. "Little Sarah."

The Brother
Saartjie. Lovely. Girl! GIRL!?

The Girl
Sir?

The Brother
Dance.

The Girl
Dance?

The Brother
Dance! Come on!
I'll clap time.

The Brother claps time.
The Girl dances.

The Man
An "African Dancing Princess?"

The Brother
The Britsll eat it up.
Oh, she'd make a splendid freak.

The Man
A freak?

The Brother
Thats what they call em
"freaks," "oddities," "curiosities."

The Man
Of course. Of course.

The Girl
Can I stop, Sir?

The Brother
No no keep up.
Faster! Ha ha!
(I still dont recognize her.)

The Man
(She might know you though.
Their kind remember everything.)

The Brother
(Ive grown a beard since then.)

The Man
Thats true.

The Brother
Stop dancing. Stop!

The Girl
Stopped.

The Brother
Girl?

The Girl
Sir.

The Brother
How would you like to go to England?

The Girl
England! Well.
"England." Whats that?

The Brother
A big town. A boat ride away.
Where the streets are paved with gold.

The Girl
Gold, Sir?

The Brother
Come to England. Dance a little.

The Girl
Dance?

The Brother
Folks watch. Folks clap. Folks pay you gold.

The Girl
Gold.

The Brother
We'll split it 50-50.

The Girl
50-50?

The Brother
Half for me half for you.
May I present to you: "The African Dancing Princess!"

The Girl
A Princess. Me?

The Brother
Like Cinderella.
Shes heard of Cinderella, right?

The Girl
A princess overnight.

The Man
Thats it.

The Brother
Yd be a sensation!

The Girl
Im a little shy.

The Brother
Say yes and we'll go tomorrow!

The Girl
Will I be the only one?

The Brother
Oh no, therell be a whole street full.

The Girl
Im shy.

The Brother
Think of it: Gold!

The Girl
Gold!

The Brother
2 yrs of work yd come back rich!

The Girl
Id come back rich!

The Brother
Yd make a mint!

The Girl
A mint! A "mint."
How much is that?

The Man
You wouldnt have to work no more.

The Girl
I would have a house.
I would hire help.
I would be rich. Very rich.
Big bags of money!

The Man
Exactly.

The Girl
I like it.

The Brother
Its settled then!

The Man
Yr a rascal, Brother.

The Girl
Do I have a choice? Id like to think on it.

The Brother
Whats there to think on? Think of it as a vacation!
2 years of work take half the take.
Come back here rich. Its settled then.

The Man
Think it over, Girl. Go on.
Think it all over.

The Brother
The Girl
The Man

The Brother
The Girl
The Man

(Rest)
(Rest)

The Girl
Hahahaha!

The Man
What an odd laugh.

The Girl
Just one question:
When do we go?

The Brother
Next stop England!

The Girl
"England?"

The Brother
England England England HO!

The Girl
"England?"

The Negro Resurrectionist
Scene #30:
She Looks Like Shes Fresh Off the Boat:

Scene 30: She Looks Like Shes Fresh Off the Boat

The Chorus of the 8 Human Wonders
Whos that?
Who knows?
Not from these parts.
She looks like shes fresh off the boat.
She looks like shes about to cry.
Go up to her say something nice. Cheer her up make her
    feel welcome.
I remember my first day here.
I didnt know which end was up.
And I had jet lag to boot.
Go to her, go on, be kind.
Go to her say something nice.
(Rest)
I dunno maybe its better to stay quiet
what can anyone say at a time like this?
"Greetings"? "Salutations"? "Everythings coming up roses"?
Right, good luck.
We could stand here and tell her some lies
or the bald truth: That her lifell go from rough to worse.
Or we could say nothing at all.
What difference will it make?
Shes sunk. Theres no escape from this place.

The Girl
Whos there.

The Chorus of the 8 Human Wonders
No one in particular.
No one you wanna know.

The Girl
Yr not the other dancing cinderellas are you?

The Chorus of the 8 Human Wonders
Hardly, Girl. We've got talents
but none youd pay to see.

The Girl
Yr singers?
Yr magicians!

The Chorus of the 8 Human Wonders
Yll find out soon enough.

The Girl
Its dark in here.
(Rest)
So this is "England."

The Chorus of the 8 Human Wonders
Bingo.

The Girl
Youve seen the golden avenues.

The Chorus of the 8 Human Wonders
Oh boy. Youve bit the big one.
I dunno maybe its better to stay quiet
What can anyone say at a time like this?
"Greetings!" "Salutations!" "Everythings coming up roses!"

The Girl
So happy to make yr aquaintance.
Ive come here to get rich.
Im an exotic dancer. Very well known at home.
My manager is at this very moment securing us a proper room.
We're planning to construct a mint, he and me together.

The Chorus of the 8 Human Wonders
Right, Girl, good luck.
We could stand here and tell her some lies

or the bald truth: That her lifell go from rough to worse.
Yr a fool, Girl!

The Girl
Yr the fools.
Yr the fools!
Huddled in the dark.
Keep yr distance! You smell!
I'd rather sit here by myself than be called names.

The Chorus of the 8 Human Wonders
I remember my first day here.
I didnt know which end was up.
And I had jet lag to boot.
Poor girl. We shoulda said nothing. Nothing at all.
What difference could it make?
Shes sunk. Sunk like the rest of us.
Welcome welcome to the club, sweetheart.
Theres no escape from this place.

The Brother enters with food.

The Brother
Here, Girl. Eat this.
It isnt much but things right now are tight.
Take it.

The Girl
Thank you.

The Brother
Here. Have some water.

The Girl
Thank you.

The Brother
Hungry?

The Girl
A little.

The Brother
Thingsll pick up soon.

The Girl
When do we get to England, Sir?

The Brother
This is England! Cant you tell?

The Girl
I wasnt sure.
(Rest)
Where are the golden streets?

The Brother
Just around that bend there.
You cant see them from here.

The Girl
Can I go out and take a look?

The Brother
No no. Dont budge.
You cant. At least not yet.

The Girl
How long will we live in this room, Sir?

The Brother
2 or 3 days at the most.
Theres an overweight bureaucrat a real fatso
who dont want you in his country.
Im oiling his palms.
Here have more water.

The Girl
Its dark in here.

The Brother
Tomorrow I'll show you the golden streets.

The Girl
Im hungry and I'm cold.
Its dark in here.

The Brother
Remember me? From way back when?
About 12 yrs ago?

The Girl
Youve growd a beard other than that
you havent changed.

The Brother
I wanted you then and I want you now.
Thats partly why we've come here.
So I can love you properly.
Not like at home.

The Girl
Home?
Love?
You oughta take me shopping. I need a new dress.
I cant be presented to society in this old thing.

The Brother
Tomorrow I'll buy you the town.
For now lift up yr skirt.
There. Thats good.

> She lifts her skirts showing her ass. He gropes her.

The Girl
I dont—

The Brother
Relax.
Presenting "The African Dancing Princess!"

The Girl
Hahahaha!
I dont think I like it here.

The Brother
Relax.
Relax.
Its going to be fantastic.

> They kiss and touch each other.
> He is more amorous than she.

(Rest)

The Negro Resurrectionist
Footnote #1:
(Rest)
Historical Extract. Category: Theatrical.
(Rest)
The year was 1810. On one end of town, in somewhat shabby circumstances, a young woman, native of the dark continent, bares her bottoms. At the same time but in a very different place, on the other end of town in fact, we witness a very different performance.
Scene 29:
Presenting: "For the Love of the Venus."
A Drama in 3 Acts. Act I, Scene 3:

Scene 29: "For the Love of the Venus." Act I, Scene 3

> A play on a stage. The Baron Docteur is the only
> person in the audience. Perhaps he sits in a chair.
> It's almost as if he's watching TV.
> The Venus stands off to the side. She watches The Baron Docteur.

The Bride-to-Be
Coffee, darling.

The Young Man
No thank you.

The Bride-to-Be
Tea.

The Young Man
No thank you.

The Bride-to-Be
Chocolate.

The Young Man
Chocolate. Mmmmm.

The Bride-to-Be
Mmmmm?

The Young Man
No *thank* you.

The Bride-to-Be
Look! Oh, what a treasure:
Bah-nah-nah.

The Young Man
You *peel* it.

The Bride-to-Be
Peel it. Novelty.

The Young Man
Uncle took Dad to Africa.
Showed Dad stuff. Blew Dads mind.
(Rest)

                           The Young Man reads from his notebook.

The Young Man
"The Man who has never been from his own home is no *Man*.
For how can a Man call himself *Man* if he has not stepped off
his own doorstep and wandered out into the world . . . Visit
the world and *Man* he will be."

[The Bride-to-Be
Canasta.
Whist?
Crazy 8s?

The Young Man
"When a Man takes his journey beyond all that to him was
hitherto the Known, when a Man packs his baggage and walks
himself beyond the Familiar, then sees he his true I; not in the
eyes of the Known but in the eyes of the Known-Not."**]**

The Bride-to-Be
You wrote me once
such lovely poetry.

The Young Man
"His place in the Great Chain of Being is then to him and to
all that set their eyes upon him, thus revealed."

The Bride-to-Be
"My Love for you is artificial
Fabricated much like this epistle."
(Rest)
Such poetry you used to write me.

The Young Man
"Beholding and Beheld as he is seen through the eyes of the
Great Known-Not—taking his rightful place among the Splend-
ors of the Universe."
(Rest)
(Rest)
"Among the Splendors of *Gods* Universe" it should be.
Dontcha think?

The Bride-to-Be
Aaahh me:
Unloved.

Curtain.
The Baron Docteur applauds.

Scene 28: Footnote #2

The Negro Resurrectionist holds fast to The Venus's arm. He
reads through The Baron Docteur's notebook.

The Negro Resurrectionist
Footnote #2:
(Rest)
Historical Extract. Category: Medical. Autopsy report:
(Rest)
"Her brain, immediately after removal, deprived of the greater
part of its membranes, weighed 38 ounces."
(Rest)
"Her spinal cord was not examined, as it was considered more
desirable to preserve the vertebral column intact. The dis-
section of her nerves, although carefully made, revealed no
important deviations from the ordinary arrangement."
(Rest)
"Her liver weighed 54 and 3/4 ounces and was of a ruinous
color and slightly fatty."
(Rest)
"Her gallbladder was small and a little dilated at the *fundus*,
being almost cylindrical when distendid with air. Length 4
inches."
(Rest)
"Her stomach was of the usual form. Small intestines measured
15 feet. Spleen was pale in color and weighed 2 and 1/4 ounces.
Her pancreas weighed 1 and 3/4 ounces. Her kidneys were large."
(Rest)

He releases The Venus's arm. She flees but doesn't get far.
She runs smack into The Mother-Showman.

*Scene 27: Presenting the Mother-Showman and Her Great
Chain of Being*

The Mother-Showman
Strip down.
Strip down come on yr filthy, Girl.
Come on lets move, thats it take off every stitch and hand it
    here and pronto!
I'll clean em for ya.
Damn its dark in here.
That scrap too around yr womans parts hand that here too.

The Girl
It dont come off
it stays. Its custom.

The Mother-Showman
Fine.
God. He wasnt lying.
You got enough here to make em come running.
Todays my lucky day.

The Girl
Whats that?

The Mother-Showman
You smell.
So smelly yll make em go running I said.
Good God.
Heres a bucket and a brush.
Take a bath its yr big day today.
Yr gonna be presented to society so to speak.
Scrub down you smell I said.

The Girl
Maam. Who are you.

The Negro Resurrectionist
Scene 27:
Presenting The Mother-Showman
and Her Great Chain of Being:

The Mother-Showman
Im yr new boss.
Mother-Showman and her 8 Amazing Human Wonders!
Yr Number 9.

The Girl
Wheres my Man?
He had a beard.

The Mother-Showman
Him? Girl, he skipped town.
Yr lucky I was passing through
good God girl he wasnt lying, you woulda starved to death or
    worse, been throwd in jail for heh
indecency. But its alright now, dear. Mother-Showmanll
    guard yr Interests.
Yr Secrets are safe with me.
Scrub.
SCRUB!

> The Girl, apart from the others, scrubs herself.
> The Mother-Showman introduces her Wonders.

The Mother-Showman
Sound the drum.

> Wonder #3 sounds the drum.

The Mother-Showman
Step right up come on come in.
Step inside come on come see
the most lowly and unfortunate beings in Gods Universe:
Mother-Showmans 9 Human Wonders will dazzle

surprise intrigue horrify and disgust.
The 9 lowest links in Gods Great Chain of Being.

The Chorus of the 8 Human Wonders
Chain Chain Chain.

The Mother-Showman
Look sad like yr misfitness hangs heavy on yr mind.
(Rest)
Come on in in see with yr own eyes what never ever
should have been allowed to live.
The 9 lowest links in Gods Great Bein Chain.

The Chorus of the 8 Human Wonders
Chain Chain Chain.

The Mother-Showman
See one for the price of a penny and a half
or all these 8 for a song!
Step inside come on come see
the ugliest creatures in creativity. Alive!
Alive! And waiting for you just inside.
Come on in in take a look
see a living misfit with yr own eyes.
Take a look at one for just a penny and a half
you can gawk as long as you like.
Waiting for yr gaze here inside
theyre all freaks and all alive.

[The Chorus of the 8 Human Wonders
When I was birthed intuh this world
our Father cursed our Mother spat.
SPAT!

The Mother-Showman
Sing!

The Chorus of the 8 Human Wonders
This face of mine thats scary
these blemishes this crooked back
this extra arm uhtop my head

this extra ear this extra leg
this fin that swims out of my rear
these blisters circling my eyes
passed down tuh me from who knows where
my existence is a curse
you can gawk for a small purse!
(Rest)
We wonder thuh world.

The Mother-Showman
Step up step in to see what God hisself dont wanna look at.
Every day all day theyre on display!
All Alive!
(Rest)
Uh hehm.
8th being from the bottom, what I call my Wonder 1: The
    Bearded Gal.
Uh woman furrier than most.
By her Mom and Pop she was rejected.
Shes thuh first freak I collected.

Wonder #1
Pull on my beard!
Its real! Its real!

The Chorus of the 8 Human Wonders
We wonder thuh world.

The Mother-Showman
After 1 comes Wonder 2 one step closer to the monkeys.
Uh Fireman who dines on flame.
He claims thuh Devil his creator
but really hails from thuh Equator.

Wonder #2
I am her most Flame-boyant child!
Im goin tuh Hell! Hell in uh handbasket!

The Mother-Showman
Next rung closer to thuh lowest: Wonder 3: Thuh Spotted Boy.
Hes covered black and white all patchy

thuh Lord could not make up his mind.
Dont get too close tuh him its catchy.

Wonder #3
The Good Lord is indecisive!
Im thuh proof!

The Chorus of the 8 Human Wonders
We wander
thuh world.

The Mother-Showman
Thuh Fat Mans next: 12 hundred pounds, uh warnin to us all.

Wonder #4
Feed me.

The Mother-Showman
And if his girth does not impress
Ive 2 ladies here joined at thuh hip.
Bornd that way theyll die that way
mano a mano lip tuh lip.

Wonders #5 and #6
Mano a mano lip tuh lip.

The Chorus of the 8 Human Wonders
We wander thuh world.

The Mother-Showman
Chain.

The Chorus of the 8 Human Wonders
Chain.
We wander thuh world: Here is thuh Reason:
Our funny looks read as High Treason.

The Mother-Showman
Jawohl Jawohl!
Step up my Wandering Wunderfuls
and show how Nature takes her toll.

Almost thuh lowest to thuh bottom is a freak called "Mr.
     Privates."
Hes from thuh South
what we carry *down here* he wears up here
in thuh place of his eyes and his nose and his mouth.

Wonder #7
Horror! Horror!
Horror! Horror!

The Chorus of the 8 Human Wonders
Chain!
Chain!

The Mother-Showman
On the bottom yesterday was the Whatsit, people, #8.
So backward that her cyclops eye
will see into yr future.

Wonder #8
Black its black!
Myeye sees black!

The Chorus of the 8 Human Wonders
Howuhbouthat?!
Howuhbouthat?!

Wonder #8
Black its black!
Myeye sees black!

The Chorus of the 8 Human Wonders
Howuhbouthat?!
Howuhbouthat?!

The Mother-Showman]
Foam rage tear at yr clothes, kids!
Show yr stuff! Dont be shy!
Pull out all thuh stops! Big Finish!
Thats it! Thats it! Make yr Mama proud!

The Wonders pull out all the stops,
then they pose in a freakish tableau.
The Girl has finished her bath.
The Negro Resurrectionist watches her.

The Venus
What you lookin at?

The Negro Resurrectionist
You.
(Rest)
Yr lovely.

The Venus
The Negro Resurrectionist
The Venus
The Negro Resurrectionist

The Mother-Showman
With yr appreciative permission
for a seperate admission
we've got a new girl: #9
"The Venus Hottentot."
She bottoms out at the bottom of the ladder
yr not a man—until youve hadder.
But truly, folks, before she showd up our little show was in
    the red
but her big bottoms friendsll surely put us safely in the black!

The Girl stands in the semidarkness. Lights blaze on her.
She is now The Venus Hottentot.
The Wonders become The Chorus of the Spectators
and gather round.

The Mother-Showman
THE VENUS HOTTENTOT
THE ONLY LIVNG CREATURE OF HER KIND IN THE
    WORLD
STEPSISTER-MONKEY TO THE GREAT VENAL
LOVE
GODDESS

AND ONLY ONE STEP UHWAY FROM YOU RIGHT NOW
COME SEE THE HOT MISS HOTTENTOT
STEP IN STEP IN
HUR-RY! HUR-RY!
HUR-RY! HUR-RY!

The Venus
The Chorus of the Spectators
The Venus
The Chorus of the Spectators
The Venus
The Chorus of the Spectators
The Venus
The Chorus of the Spectators

(Rest)

The Venus
Oh, God:
Unloved.
(Rest)

The Negro Resurrectionist
Footnote #3:
Historical Extract. Category: Literary. From Robert Chambers's
Book of Days:
(Rest)
"Early in the present century a poor wretched woman was
exhibited in England under the appellation of *The Hottentot
Venus*. The year was 1810. With an intensely ugly figure, dis-
torted beyond all European notions of beauty, she was said by
those to whom she belonged to possess precisely the kind of
shape which is most admired among her countrymen, the
Hottentots."
(Rest)
The year was 1810, three years after the Bill for the Abolition
of the Slave-Trade had been passed in Parliament, and among
protests and denials, horror and fascination, The Venus show
went on.
(Rest)

The Venus
The Chorus of the Spectators
The Venus
The Chorus of the Spectators
The Venus

Spectator #1
Eeeeeeeeeeeeeeeeeeeeeeeeeeeeeeeeeeeeeeeeeeeeee!

The Mother-Showman
Get used to it, Girl.
(Rest)

The Negro Resurrectionist
Scene 26:
From "For the Love of the Venus." Act II, Scene 9:

Scene 26: "For the Love of the Venus." Act II, Scene 9

As before, The Baron Docteur is its only audience,
and The Venus watches him.

The Bride-to-Be
Eeeeeeeeeeeeeeeeeee
he doesnt care
uh whit uhbout meeee.

The Mother
Dont be a gumball, child.

The Bride-to-Be
He turns down tea.
He turns down coffee.
He will not take a turn in the park with me.
He will not hold my hand.

The Mother
Have you tried whist? He loves his whist.

The Bride-to-Be
He used to leave me
poetry
in thuh knot of thuh tree in thuh front of my house.

The Mother
Have you tried canasta?

The Bride-to-Be
"My love for you, My Love, is artificial

Fabricated much like this epistle . . ."
(Rest)
"My Love, My Love, My Love, My Love—"
No more rhymes.
Now he writes *tracts*.
Prose essays on *(Africaaaaah!)*

The Mother
There there Girl dont cry.
Have faith in Love. Wipe your nose.
There there thats nice.

The Bride-to-Be
Aaaah me: Unloved.

Tableau.
The Baron Docteur applauds.
Curtain.

The Negro Resurrectionist
Counting Down/Counting the Take:

Scene 25: Counting Down/Counting the Take

Spectator #1
Eeeeeeeeeeeeeeeeeeeeeeeeee!

The Mother-Showman
Get used to it, Girl
we're gonna be rich.
(Rest)
Can you count?

The Venus
I can count.

The Mother-Showman
That puts you a bit above the rest.
But thats our secret.

The Negro Resurrectionist
Scene 25:

The Mother-Showman
10-20-30-40
50-60-70-80-90:

The Venus
1.

The Mother-Showman
10-20-30-40
50-60-70-80-90:

The Venus
2.

The Mother-Showman
10-20-30-40
50-60-70-80-90:

The Venus
3.

The Mother-Showman
10-20-30-40
50-60-70-80-90:

The Venus
4.

The Mother-Showman
10-20-30-40
50-60-70-80-90:

The Venus
5.

The Mother-Showman
10-20-30-40
50-60-70-80-90:

The Venus
6.
(Rest)

The Mother-Showman
9 ugly mouths to feed.
Plus my own.
We didnt do too bad today.
Hottentot, yr a godsend!

The Negro Resurrectionist
31
30
29
28
27
26
25
24:

Scene 24: *"But No One Ever Noticed/Her Face Was Streamed with Tears"*

The Chorus of the 8 Human Wonders
Ive been in this line of work for years
and yet everytime the crowds gather and the lights flash up
I freak out.
My first 5 months in this racket were like hell.
I didnt sleep I didnt eat my teeth were chattering nonstop.
That girl they call The Venus H. is holding up
holding up pretty well I think. And her crowds have been
   stupendous.
(Some audience is better than none at all and since shes come
we're in another economic bracket.) Stupendous!
Stupendous! Still: Shes got that far away look in her eye
that look of someone who dont know thuh score.
She signed on for 2 years "only 19 months to go" shes thinking.
But should I tell her? Uh uhnn, I havent got the heart to say:
"Oh, Venus H., there is absolutely no escape."
(Rest)
(Rest)

> An enormous banner unfurls. It reads
> "The Venus Hottentot" and bears her likeness.
> The Venus center stage. The Wonders in the background.

The Mother-Showman
Turn to the side, Girl.
Let em see! Let em see!
(Rest)
What a fat ass, huh?!
Oh yes, this girls thuh Missin Link herself.

Come on inside and allow her to reveal to you the Great and
     Horrid Wonder
of her great heathen buttocks.
Thuh Missing Link, Ladies and Gentlemen: Thuh Venus
     Hottentot:
Uh warnin tuh us all.
Right this way.
(Rest)
Sure is slow today.
No one around for miles.
Lets see:
(Rest)
Plucked her from thuh Fertile Crescent
from thuh Fertile Crescent with my own bare hands!
Ripped her off thuh mammoth lap of uh mammoth ape!
She was uh (((*keeping house for him*))). Folks, The Venus
     Hottentot!
(Rest)
Yr standing there with yr lips pokin out
like uh wooden lady on uh wooden ship
look uhlive
smile or somethin
jesus
stroke yr feathers
smoke yr pipe.
(Rest)
Been with us in civilization for a mere 5 months. Teached
     her all she knows.
Look! Shes got talents!
(Rest)
Walk, Girl.

                                        The Venus walks about.

The Mother-Showman
WHAT A BLACKSIDE! OOOH LA LA!
STEP IN!
STEP IN STEP IN STEP IN STEP IN!
(Rest)
(Rest)
Dry as a bone today.

(Rest)
Dance or something.

The Venus
Dance?

The Mother-Showman
Dance. Go on Girl and the other uglies you all too.
I'll clap time.
DANCE!

> The Mother-Showman claps time.
> The Venus and The Wonders dance.
>
> Suddenly The Wonders disappear.

The Negro Resurrectionist
Footnote #4:
Historical Extract. Category: Newspaper Advertisements.
AN ADVERTISING BILL:
From Daniel Lysons *Collectanea: A Collection of Advertisements and Paragraphs from the Newspapers Relating to Various Subjects* (London, 1809).

"Parties of 12 and upwards, may be accommodated with a Private Exhibition of The Hottentot . . . between 7 and 8 o'clock in the evening, by giving notice to the Door-Keeper the day previous.

"The Hottentot may also be viewed by single parties with no advance notice from 10 in the morning until 10 in the evening. Mondays through Saturdays. No advance notice is necessary.

"A Woman will attend (if required)."

> The Mother-Showman is still clapping time.
> The Venus is still dancing.
> Spectator #2 wanders in to watch. He hands over a coin.

The Mother-Showman
Good morning, Sir!
Good morning!
A thousand thanks a million pleasantries
we do appreciate yr audience.

> The Mother-Showman out of breath stops clapping.
> The Venus stops dancing.
> Spectator #2 pays some more.

The Mother-Showman
What a bucket!
What a bum!
What a spanker!
Never seen the likes of that, I'll bet.
Go on Sir, go on.
Feel her if you like.

> He takes a feel. He wanders off.
> The Mother-Showman wets her finger and tests
> the wind direction.

The Mother-Showman
Look extra pitiful, Girl. Yeah thats it.
(Rest)
Ladies and Gents are you feeling lowly?
Down in the dumps?
Perhaps yr feelin that yr life is all for naught? Ive felt that
    way myself at times.
Come on inside and get yr spirits lifted.
One look at thisll make you feel like a King!

> Several Spectators wander in.

The Mother-Showman
Ladies and Gents: The Venus Hottentot
Shes been in civilization a whole year and still hasnt learnd
    nothin!
The very lowest rung on Our Lords Great Evolutionary Ladder!
Observe: I kick her like I kick my dog!

> The Mother-Showman kicks The Venus repeatedly. The act
> has the feel of professional wrestling but also looks real.

The Mother-Showman	**The Venus**
Aaaah!	Oh!
Aaaah!	Ah!
Aaaah!	Oh!

Out of breath again, The Mother-Showman stops to rest.

The Mother-Showman
Whew. Thats hard work lemmie tell ya.
I need a rest. Hhh.
Paw her folks. Hands on. Go on have yr pleasure.
Her heathen shame is real.

The Spectators paw The Venus.

The Mother-Showman
Thuh kicks is native for them Hottentots.
When I was down there in their hot home.
As Gods my witness Kickin Kickin
Kickin all day Kickin at eachother
thats just their way!
They do one kick for our "move uhbout."
2 kicks means uh well "pass thuh meat."
They mix it with thuh toes n heel: Uh whole language of kicks
very sophisticated
for them of course.
(Rest)
Verify me, Venus.
(Go on, Girl, nod and back me up.)
See? I speak the truth!
Mother-Showman does not lie.
Stand up now, Girl.
Let em see you in yr alltogether.
Stand up thats it let Mother help ya.
Lets give these folks their moneys worth.
Stand still. In profile. There thats nice.
Ladies and Gents:
The Hottentots best angle.

The Chorus of the Spectators
The Venus
The Mother-Showman
The Chorus of the Spectators
The Venus
The Mother-Showman
The Chorus of the Spectators
The Venus
The Mother-Showman

(Rest)

The Chorus of the Spectators errupts in wild laughter.

The Chorus of the Spectators

HAHAHAHAHAHAHAHAHAHAHAHAHHAHAHAHAHA
HAHAHHAHAHAHAHHAHAHAHAHHAHAHAHAHA
HAHAHAHAHAHAHAHAHAHAHAHAHAHAHHAHA
HHAHA.

The Venus
The Venus
The Venus

The Venus
Hahahahahahahaha!

The Negro Resurrectionist
Footnote #5:
Historical Extract. Category: Literary. From *The Life of One Called the Venus Hottentot As Told By Herself:*
(Rest)
"The things they noticed were quite various
but no one ever noticed that her face was streamed with tears."
(Rest)
Scene 23:
From "For the Love of the Venus." Act II, Scene 10:

Scene 23: "For the Love of the Venus." Act II, Scene 10

Again, The Baron Docteur is the only audience.
The Venus watches him.

The Father
Youre in uh pickle Young Man
an absolute pickle

The Uncle
Nabsolute pickle no question Boy.

The Father
Marry yr girl, Boy and then
Unclell take ya to Timbuktu
if Timbuktus yr yen.

The Young Man
Timbuktu?
(Rest)
A Man to be a Man must know Unknowns! So
if The Man cant sail to the Unknown I guess
the Unknown will sail to The Man. So!
Im all decided:
Before I wed, Uncle, I'd like you to procure for me an oddity.
I wanna love
something Wild.

The Father
The Uncle
The Young Man

The Uncle
Be a little more specific.

The Young Man
In the paper yesterday:
"In 2 weeks time
for one week only"
something called "The Hottentot Venus"
Uncle. Get her for me somehow.

The Father and The Uncle
Heh. Heh.
Heh. Heh.

The Young Man
Im all decided.

The Father
(Make sure shes not *too* strange, Brother.
Brother, make sure shes clean.)

The Uncle
In 2 weeks time!
I will present to you, Young Man:
New Love!

> The Father, The Uncle and The Young Man in Tableau.
> The Baron Docteur applauds.
> Curtain.

Scene 22: Counting the Take/The Deal That Was

The Venus
10-20-30-40
50-60-70-80-90:

The Mother-Showman
22.

The Venus
10-20-30-40
50-60-70-80-90:

The Mother-Showman
23.

The Venus
10-20-30-40
50-60-70-80-90:

The Mother-Showman
24.

The Venus
10-20-30-40
50-60-70-80-90:

The Mother-Showman
25.

The Venus
You hit me hard the other day.

The Mother-Showman
Mothers sorry.

The Venus
We should spruce up our act.
I could speak for them.
Say a little poem or something.

The Mother-Showman
Count!

The Venus
You could pretend to teach me and I would learn
before their very eyes.

The Mother-Showman
Yr a Negro native with a most remarkable spanker.
Thats what they pay for.
Their eyes are hot for yr tot-tot.
Theres the poetry.

The Venus
We should expand.

The Mother-Showman
Count!!

The Venus
(Rest)
10-20-30-40
50-60-70-80-90:

The Mother-Showman
26.

The Venus
10-20-30-40
50-60-70-80-90:

The Mother-Showman
27.

The Venus
10-20-30-40
50-60-70-80-90:

The Mother-Showman
28.

The Venus
10-20-30-40
50-60-70-80-90:

The Mother-Showman
29.

The Venus
10-20-30-40
50-60-70-80-90:

The Mother-Showman
30.

The Venus
10-20-30-40
50-60-70-80-90:

The Mother-Showman
31. And change.
Hhhhh.
We didnt do too bad today.
(Rest)
(Rest)
Lets see now:

The Mother-Showman consults her map.

The Mother-Showman
Town X to Town Y Town Y to Town Z.
Town Z to Town A Town A to Town B.
Town B to Town C then back to Town X then off
to Town hmmmmm.

The Venus
The Mother-Showman
The Venus

The Mother-Showman
Dont steal from me, Girl.
Yll go to hell for it.

The Venus
Hell?

The Mother-Showman
Christian talk. Fire and brimstone and Satan himself.
Very hot.

The Venus
Oh.

The Mother-Showman
Put thuh money back.

The Venus
You pay us each 5 coins a week.
We're all paid equal
but we dont draw equal.

The Mother-Showman
Its past yr bedtime, Daughter.

The Venus
Im thuh one they come to see.
Im thuh main attraction.
Yr other freaks r 2nd fiddles.

The Mother-Showman
Oh boy: Uh Diva.

The Venus
I should get 50 uh week.
Plus better food, uh lock on my door and uh new dress now
  n then.

The Mother-Showman
You should get some sleep, Girl.
I wake you up early and you never like it.

The Venus
50 uh week good food locked door new clothes say its a deal.

The Mother-Showman
Go to hell.

The Venus
40 then, the clothes and my own room. Forget the food.

The Mother-Showman
Nothin doin, Lovely.

The Venus
30.

The Mother-Showman
Nope.

The Venus
Im leaving then.

The Mother-Showman
Where to?

The Venus
Home.

The Mother-Showman
But yr not yet rich and famous.

The Venus
Im not?

The Mother-Showman
Yr a little known in certain circles but you havent made yr
    fortune.
Go back home and folks will laugh.
Hahahaha.
Stay.

The Venus
No.
I'll set up shop and show myself.
Be my own Boss make my own mint.

The Mother-Showman
Youd walk out on yr mother?

The Venus
My time with you is spent.
2 yrs work
half the take for take-home pay, Im due at least a thousand
    coins!
That was the deal.

The Mother-Showman
That deal you didnt make with me, Love.
You made yr bargin with a man Ive never met!
For all I know youve made him up.
Yeah, yr lyin and tryin to swindle yr poor Mother
out of her retirement.

The Venus
2 yrs work
half the take
him and me were agreed.
Hand it over.

The Mother-Showman
Nothin doin.

The Venus
Im out of here.
I'll make my own mark.
Im all decided.

The Mother-Showman
"Im all decided" oooh la la.
Could it be Ive been showing you all wrong?
Christ I thought yr name was "Venus" but, Lord of mercy,
yr the Queen of Fucking Sheeba.

The Venus
Hand it over.

The Mother-Showman
Nope.
Go to bed.

The Venus
I want whats mine!

The Mother-Showman
They dont let your kind run loose in the streets
much less set up their own shops.

The Venus
Gimmie!

The Mother-Showman
You could be arrested.
You need Mothers protection.

The Venus
GIMMMMMIE!

The Mother-Showman
Dont push me, Sweetie.
Next doors a smoky pub
full of drunken men.
I just may invite them in
one at a time
and let them fuck yr brains out.

The Venus
They do it anyway.
(Rest)
(Rest)

The Mother-Showman
Well.
Its the same
for all of us, Love.
(Rest)

I love you like a daughter.
We're yr family now.
If you go off we'd miss you
and besides we may go under.

The Venus
They come in drunken when yr sleeping.
(Rest)
I wanna go.
Please.

The Mother-Showman
Home?

The Venus
No.
Not home.

The Mother-Showman
Where to, then?

The Venus
Innywhere.

The Mother-Showman
Sad to say, Girl, but you cant
and its the same for all of us.
The Law wants to shut us down
we create too many "disturbances" so
we gotta move about go hopping you know town to town.
A Whirlwind Tour! 100 cities in as many nights! Ive
    planned it out.
It looks like fun.
Yll see the world!

The Venus
No—

The Mother-Showman
Relax.
Relax.
Its going to be fantastic.

Scene 21: The Whirlwind Tour

During this scene The Baron Docteur watches The Venus and
the others from his chair. He grows more and
more interested and watches more and more intently.
The Venus, The Mother-Showman and The Chorus of the
8 Human Wonders stand in a knot. They are traveling.

The Negro Resurrectionist
Town A! Town B! Town C! Town E!
Town 25! Town 36! Town 42! Town 69!

[The Chorus of the 8 Human Wonders
Legend has it that The Girl was sent away from home.
Those who sent her said she couldnt return for a thousand yrs.
Even though she was strong of heart even she doubted she
    would live that long.
After 500 years they allowed her to ask a question.
She wanted to know what her crime had been.
Simple: You wanted to go away once.
9 hundred 99 of the years were finally up
just one more year to go.
She had in all that time circled the globe twice on foot
saw 12 hundred thousand cities
and had a lover or 2 in every port.
She spent her last year of banishment living in a cave carved out
outside the city wall.
She spent that whole year longing not looking but longing
    not looking.
They let her go home right on time
all of her friends had died and well
she didnt recognize the place.]

The Negro Resurrectionist

Town R! Town U! Town E! Town Q!	**The Venus**
Town 58! Town 64! Town 85! Town 99!	**The Mother-Showman**
(Rest)	**The Venus**
(Rest)	**The Mother-Showman**
Town A! Town B! Town C! Town E!	**The Venus**
Town 25! Town 36! Town 42! Town 69!	**The Mother-Showman**
(Rest)	**The Venus**
Town R! Town U! Town E! Town Q!	**The Mother-Showman**
Town 58! Town 64! Town 85! Town 99!	**The Venus**

The Venus
How many towns till we get home?!

The Mother-Showman
Presenting:
Presenting:
Presenting:
THE VENUS HOTTENTOT!
Love gone all wrong, if you will.
Uh warning to us all.
Gentlemen, Ladies, get yrselves a good long look.
Kiddies push yr ways up front.

The Chorus of the Spectators
The Venus

The Chorus of the Spectators
(Rest)
Ooooooooooooooooooooooooooooh!
(Rest)
(Rest)
Aaaaaaaaaaaaaaaaaaaaaaaaaaaaaaaah!
(Rest)
(Rest)

The Negro Resurrectionist
Town 10! Town 3!
Town R! Town Z!
Town X!

The Mother-Showman
Uh gift of chocklut is customary.
Place yr treats at her feets and watch her feed.

The Negro Resurrectionist

Town R! Town U! Town E! Town Q!	**The Venus**
Town 58! Town 64! Town 85! Town 99!	**The Mother-Showman**
(Rest)	**The Venus**
(Rest)	**The Mother-Showman**
Town A! Town B! Town C! Town E!	**The Venus**
Town 25! Town 36! Town 42! Town 69!	**The Mother-Showman**
(Rest)	**The Venus**
Town R! Town U! Town E! Town Q!	**The Mother-Showman**
Town 58! Town 64! Town 85! Town 99!	**The Venus**

The Venus
How many towns till we get home?

[The Chorus of the Spectators
Legend has it that The Girl was sent away from home.
Those who sent her said she couldnt return for a thousand yrs.
Even though she was strong of heart even she doubted she
   would live that long.
After 500 years they allowed her to ask a question.
She wanted to know what her crime had been.
Simple: You wanted to go away once.
9 hundred 98 of the years were finally up
just 2 short years to go.
She had in all that time circled the globe twice on foot
saw 12 hundred thousand cities
and had a lover or 2 in every port.
She spent her last 2 years of banishment living in a cave
   carved out
outside the city wall.
She spent those 2 years longing not looking but longing not
   looking.

They let her go home right on time
all of her friends had died and well
she didnt recognize the place.**]**

The Negro Resurrectionist
Town R! Town U! Town E! Town Q!
Town 58! Town 64! Town 85! Town 99!
(Rest)
Town M! Town O! Town P! Town S!
Town 3! Town 5! Town 4! Town 9!

> The Baron Docteur is out of his chair and watching
> The Venus. He is transfixed.

The Venus
The Chorus of the Spectators

> The Chorus of the Spectators bursts into riot.
> They beat The Venus's cage with sticks.
> They also beat The Mother-Showman.

The Baron Docteur
Order! Order! Order! Order!

*Scene 20A: The Venus Hottentot Before the Law
(Footnote #6: Historical Extract: Musical. From R. Toole-
Scott's "The Circus and the Allied Arts")*

The Negro Resurrectionist
(Rest)
A Song of The Hottentot ladie and her day in court and what
the judges did therein.

As The Negro Resurrectionist sings, The Chorus of the
Spectators leads The Venus to a jail cell and then transforms
themselves into The Chorus of the Court.

The Negro Resurrectionist
Have you heard about
the rump she has (though strange it be).
Large as a cauldron pot?
This is why men go to see
The Venus Hottentot.

She showd her butts for many a day,
and eke for many a night;
till fights broke out in our dear streets
now, this was not alright.
Some said this was with her goodwill
some said that this was not.
All asked why they did use so ill
this lady Hottentot.

At last the sober folks stood forth
And into Court they took her.
To thus determine if she liked
for everyone to look her.

So they questioned the girl in court
along with many more
to learn if she did money get
and what xactly was the score?
Who having finished their intent
they visited the spot
and said twas done with full consent
of the fair Hottentot.

When speaking free from all alarm
the whole she does deride
and says she thinks there is no great harm
in showing her backside.

And now good people let us go
to see this wondrous sight.
We'll have uh gawk, toss her uh sweet
such recreation cant be beat.
Lets not be critical of what Loves got
cause lookin at her past-tense end
delights so much The Hottentot.

The Chorus is now The Chorus of the Court.

Scene 20B: The Venus Hottentot Before the Law (continued)
(Historical Extract)

The Chorus of the Court
We representatives of the Law
have hauled into Court the case
of a most unfortunate female, who has been known to
    exhibit herself
to the view of the Public
in a manner offensive to decency and disgraceful to our country.
This Court wonders if she is at inny time
under the control of others, or some dark force, some say,
    black magic
making her exhibition against her will.
We ask 2 questions: Is she or was she ever indecent? And at
    inny time held against her will?
We do not wish to send her adrift in the world without
    asylum of a friend
a friend ready to receive and protect her.
But to the honor and credit of this country,
she will not find herslf without friends and protection
even if she may be employed to expose herself
in a most disgraceful manner, however,
the Court intends to interfere and
receive her immediately under its protection;
for the purpose of restoring her to her own friends and her
    own country
so that she not become a burden to the state and contribute
    to our growing social ills.
(Rest)
Lets get this show on the road.
We begin with a writ of *Habeas Corpus*.

Scene 20C: The Venus Hottentot Before the Law (continued)
(Dictionary Extract: From Webster's Ninth New Collegiate
Dictionary, page 545)

Apart from the "courtroom" The Venus sits in a jail cell.

The Venus
(Rest)
Habeas Corpus. Literally: "You should have the body" for
submitting. Any of several common-law writs issued to bring
the body before the court or the judge.

Scene 20D: The Venus Hottentot Before the Law (continued)
(First Witness)

The Chorus of the Court
First Witness!

The Chorus Leader
We call for the testimony of her present Keeper
one called "The Mother-Showman."
Mother-Showman, take the stand!

The Mother-Showman
The one called The Mother-Showman is
unavailable for comment.

The Chorus of the Court
Where is she? Find her!

The Mother-Showman
Shes got 9 ugly mouths to feed.
She works day in day out, folks.
As to any questions
concerning the Goddess Venus H.
if Mothers been unkind she swears to mend her evil ways!

The Chorus of the Court
Haul her in here!

The Mother-Showman
Mama submits
a certificate of baptism of the so-called Venus Hottentot
as proof that I take good care of her.

The Chorus Leader
Hmmmmmm. Interesting.
Submit the certificate of baptism as Exhibit A.

Scene 20E: The Venus Hottentot Before the Law (continued)
(Historical Extract: Exhibit A)

The Negro Resurrectionist
Exhibit A: The Certificate of Baptism

The Venus
(Rest)
Baptised 1 December 1811. The ceremony took place in Manchester, the clergyman being Reverend Joshua Brookes. The certificate of baptism is preserved in Paris. It states: "December 1. Sarah Baartman a Female Hottentot from the Colony of the Cape of Good Hope, born on the Borders of Caffraria, baptized this day by Permission of the Lord Bishop."

Scene 20F: The Venus Hottentot Before the Law (continued)
(Witness 1 and Witness 2)

The Chorus of the Court
Lets get uh witness on the stand!

> The Chorus ejects one of its members: Witness #1.

The Negro Resurrectionist
1st Witness:
Historical Extract: From a Mr. Hall, Member of Society:

Witness #1
I saw her, oh several times.
Call me and my Mrs. her regulars. She was always
standing on a stage, 2 feet high, clothed in a light dress,
a dress thuh color of her own skin.
She looked, well, naked, kin I say that?
The whole place smelled of shit.
She didnt speak at all.
My Mrs. always fainted.

> The Chorus ejects another member: Witness #2.
> Witness #1 rejoins The Chorus.

The Chorus of the Court
Whos next?! Whos next!?

The Negro Resurrectionist
2nd Witness:
Historical Extract: Mr. Charles Mathewes visited The Venus
and related this scene to his now widow:

Witness #2
Im a widow.

The Chorus of the Court
Widow, tell us whatcha seen.

Witness #2
I saw nothin.
Hearsay only.
2nd hand.

The Chorus of the Court
Thatll do.
Spit it out.

Witness #2
Good people, Im uh Widow.
My dear man was fond of sights and before he died
he viewd The Venus H.
He related it to me this way:
"She was surrounded by many persons, some *females*!
One pinched her, another walked round her;
one gentleman *poked* her with his cane;
uh *lady* used her parasol to see if all was, as she called it,
    '*natural.*'
Through all of this the creature didnt speak.
Maybe uh sigh or 2 maybe when she seemed inclined to
    protest the pawing."
She once handed my man a feather from her head.
Theyre said to bring good luck.
"A fight ensued. 3 men died. Uh little boy went mad. Uh
    woman lost her child."
My man escaped with thuh feather intact.
"Poor Creature."
"Very extraordinary indeed!"
"This is a sight which makes me melancholy!"
My husbands words exactly.
He was home standing by the window. I can see him now.
And then he walked away from me, deep in thought,
and then, totally forgetting his compassion, shouted loud:
"Good God what butts!"
(Rest)
Thuh shock of her killed him, I think,
cause 2 days later he was dead.
Ive thrown thuh feather away.

Scene 20G: The Venus Hottentot Before the Law (continued)
(Exhibit B)

The Venus
Exhibit B:
A feather from the head of the
so-called Venus H.
The feathers were said to bring good luck—
when stroked such feathers cured infertility.
When ground and ingested these same feathers proved
a brilliant aphrodisiac.

Scene 20H: The Venus Hottentot Before the Law (continued)
(Witness 3 and Witness 4)

The Chorus Leader
Let the Widow step down.
Who's next? Who's next?

The Chorus of the Court
We call to the stand
the man who watches her from afar:
The Baron Docteur.

The Baron Docteur
The Baron Docteur is
unavailable for comment.

The Chorus of the Court
Outrage! ItsanOutrage!

The Baron Docteur
Im speaking on The Venus subject at a conference.
Yll have to wait till then.

The Chorus of the Court
Outrage! ItsanOutrage!
Lets get someone anyone on the stand!

> They eject another member: Witness #3.

The Chorus Leader
We call to the stand
a noted Abolitionist.

71

Witness #3

I am a noted abolitionist.

The Negro Resurrectionist

Historical Extract. Category: Journalistic.
A letter of protest appearing in *The Morning Chronicle,
Friday, 12 October 1810:*

Witness #3

"Sir,
As a friend to liberty, in every situation of life, I cannot help
calling your attention to a subject, which I am sure need only
be noticed by you to insure your immediate obesevation and
comment. I allude to that wretched object advertised and
publicly shown for money—'The Hottentot Venus.' This, Sir,
is a wretched creature—an inhabitant of the interior of Africa,
who has been brought here as a subject for the curiosity of this
country, for 2 cents a-head. Her keeper is the only gainer. I
am no advocate of these sights, on the contrary, I think it base
in the extreme, that *any* human beings should be thus
exposed! It is contrary to every principle of morality and good
order as this exhibition connects the same offense to public
decency with that most horrid of all situations, *Slavery*."

Witness #4

Equal time! Equal time!
I represent a man who knows!

The Negro Resurrectionist

A reply appearing in *The Morning Chronicle, 23 October 1810.*

Witness #4

"Since the English last took possession of the colonies, we
have been consistently solicited to bring to this country, subjects well worthy of the attention of the Virtuoso, and the curious in general. The girl in question fits this description and
interest in her has been fully proved by the approbation of
some of the First Rank and Chief Literati of the kingdom, who
saw her previous to her being publicly exhibited. And pray,
has she not as good a right to exhibit herself as the Famous
Irish Giant or the renowned Dogfaced Dancing Dwarf?!?!"

The Chorus of the Court
Thank you, Sirs.
You may step down.
The Court grants the writ of *Habeas Corpus*.
Bring up the body of this female.

Scene 20I: The Venus Hottentot Before the Law (continued)
(Historical Extract)

                              The Venus comes out of her cage.

The Chorus of the Court
We call The Venus Hottentot.

The Venus
Im called The Venus Hottentot.

The Chorus of the Court
She speaks!!
(Rest)
Simple questions first.
Who are you?
Where are you from?
Any family?
Are you happy?
Are you a witch?
Were you ever beaten?
Did you like it was it good?
Do you wanna go home?
If so, when?! If so, when?!
Answer, come on, spit it out!

The Venus
The Venus
The Venus

The Venus
The Venus Hottentot
is unavailable for comment.

The Chorus of the Court
Dont push us, Girl!
We could lock you up for life!
Answer this:
Are you here of yr own free will
or are you under some restraint?

The Venus
Im here to make a mint.

The Chorus of the Court
Hubba-Hubba-Hubba-Hubba.
(Order-order-order-order.)

The Venus
After all Ive gone through so far
to go home penniless would be disgraceful.

The Chorus of the Court
Is poverty more disgraceful than nakedness?
We think not!

The Chorus Leader
Shut her down!
Send her home!

The Venus
Good people. Let me stay.

The Chorus Leader
No way!
Her kind bear Gods bad mark and, baptised or not,
they blacken-up the honor of our fair country.
Get her out of here!

The Chorus of the Court
Shut her down!
Send her home!

The Venus
No!

Please. Good good honest people.
If I bear thuh bad mark what better way to cleanse it off?
Showing my sinful person as a caution to you all could,
in the Lords eyes, be a sort of repentance
and I could wash off my dark mark.
I came here black.
Give me the chance to leave here white.

The Chorus of the Court
Hmmmmmmmmmm.
Her words strike a deep chord.
(Rest)
One more question, Girl, uh:
Have you ever been indecent?

The Chorus of the Court
The Venus
The Chorus of the Court

The Venus
(Rest)
"Indecent?"

The Chorus of the Court
Nasty.

The Venus
Never.
No. I am just me.

The Chorus of the Court
Whats that supposed to mean?!?!

The Venus
To hide yr shame is evil.
I show mine. Would you like to see?

The Chorus of the Court
Outrage! Ssanoutrage!
Outrage! Ssanoutrage!
(Order order order order.)

(Order order order order.)
God! Weve got
a lot to think about.
Recess! Recess!
Lets take uh break.

They huddle in a knot.

The Negro Resurrectionist
The year was 1810, three years after the Bill for the Abolition
of the Slave-Trade had been passed in Parliament. Among
protests and denials, horror and fascination the show went on.
(Rest)
Scene 20J:

Scene 20J: The Venus Hottentot Before the Law (conclusion)
(Historical Extract)

The Chorus of the Court

Hear ye hear ye hear
All rise and hear our ruling:
It appears to the Court
that the person on whose behalf this suit was brought
lives under no restraint.
Her exhibition sounds indecent
but look at her now, shes nicely dressed.
It is clear shes got grand plots and plans
to make her mark and her mint by playing outside the
    bounds so that we find
her person much depraved but she sez her show is part of
    Gods great plan
and we buy that.
Besides she has the right to make her mark just like the
    Dancing Irish Dwarf
and she seems well fed.
At this time the Court rules
not to rule.
(Rest)
In closing, whatever happens to her
we should note that
it is very much to the credit of our great country
that even a female Hottentot can find a court to review her status.
(Rest)
(Rest)
HAHAHAHAHAHAHAHAHAHHAHAHAHAHHAHAHA
HAHAHAHAHAHAHAHAHAHAHAHAHAHHAHAH
HAHAHA.

The Baron Docteur
Order! Order!
Order! Order!

The Chorus of the Court vanishes.

The Negro Resurrectionist
Scene 19:
A Scene of Love
(?):

Scene 19: A Scene of Love (?)

The Venus
The Baron Docteur
The Venus
The Baron Docteur
The Venus
The Baron Docteur
The Venus
The Baron Docteur
The Venus

Scene 18: She Always Was My Favorite Child

The Baron Docteur
You show The Venus Hottentot?

The Mother-Showman
Thats right.
Thought up her name and everything.
Im always by her side.

The Baron Docteur
I'd like to take her off yr hands.

The Mother-Showman
You would, huh?
To what purpose?

The Baron Docteur
Thats none of yr business.

The Mother-Showman
You want her for a servant, right?
Shes got talents but not on that line.
Besides. Shes wild. Pure heathen.
May revert as they call it inny minute.
Bite you square in thuh face.
My ears thuh proof of that.
Shes no servin girl, Sir. Sorry.

The Baron Docteur
Im a doctor.

The Mother-Showman
Shes my prize Doc.

The Baron Docteur
She must be a handful to maintain.

The Mother-Showman
That she is.

The Baron Docteur
Her appeal wont last much longer.
The crowds are looking skimpy.

The Mother-Showman
Thats my business.

The Baron Docteur
Come on. How much.

The Mother-Showman
Long term
or short term rental?

The Baron Docteur
Permanent.
Name yr price.

The Mother-Showman
The Mother-Showman

The Mother-Showman
I might retire afterall.
What do you want her for?

The Baron Docteur
Thats not yr concern.
How much?

The Mother-Showman
The Baron Docteur

The Baron Docteur
Ive watched you with her, woman.
You kick her like I kick my dog!

The Mother-Showman
The Baron Docteur
The Mother-Showman
The Baron Docteur

(Rest)

The Mother-Showman
We seem to have an understanding.

The Baron Docteur
How much.

The Mother-Showman
A lot.

The Baron Docteur
Ok.

The Mother-Showman
A ton.

The Baron Docteur
Alright.

The Mother-Showman
A mint!
A fortune!
Fort Knox!

The Baron Docteur
Here here take it take it.

The Mother-Showman
My retirement!
(Rest)
Whatll you do with her? Im curious.

The Baron Docteur
Get her out of that filthy cage for one.
Teach her French. Who knows.

The Mother-Showman
Be good to her, Sir.
We sure will miss her.
She always was my favorite child.

Scene 17: You Look Like You Need a Vacation

The Negro Resurrectionist
Scene 17:

The Chorus of the 8 Human Wonders
Ive been in this line of work for years and years
and every time the crowds gather
and the lights flash on me
I freak out.
That girl they call The Venus, The Venus Hottentot, shes
    holding up, well,
pretty well: Stupendous. Stupendous. Still:
Shes got that far away look in her eye.
That look of someone who dont know whats in store.
She signed on for 2 years. "One more month," shes thinking.
"One more month one more month one more month."
But should I tell her? No, I havent got the balls to say:
Lovely Venus, with yr looks theres absolutely no escape.

The Venus
Whos there.

The Baron Docteur
A friend.
Im yr biggest fan.

The Venus
No—

The Baron Docteur
I find you fascinating.

The Venus
No—

The Baron Docteur
Not like that, Girl.
Im a doctor.
"Doctor."
Understand?

The Venus
The Baron Docteur

(Rest)

The Venus
I understand.

The Baron Docteur
Ive brought you chockluts. Here.
You like?

He gives her a red heart box of chocolates.

The Venus
I like.

The Baron Docteur
Well.
Lets have a look.
Stand still stand still, sweetheart
I'll orbit.
Dont start Ive doctors eyes and hands.
Well.
Extraordinary.
(Rest)
(Rest)
Sweetheart, how would you like to go to Paris?

The Venus
"Paris." Well.
"Paris."
Whats that?

The Baron Docteur
A big town!
Only a short boat ride away!

The Venus
"Paris."

The Baron Docteur
"The City of Lights!"
I'd teach you French.

The Venus
"French."

The Baron Docteur
Ive paid yr Mother off.
Yd have a clean room.
Mix with my associates.
Move in a better circle.

The Venus
"Circle"
(Rest)
Yr hands. Theyre clean.
Are you rich?

The Baron Docteur
Very.

The Venus
. I like rich.

The Baron Docteur
Its settled then.
I find you quite phenomenal.
Hell, you look like you need a vacation. Say "yes!"
Say "yes" and we'll leave this minute.

The Venus
Do I have a choice?

The Baron Docteur
Yes. God. Of course.

The Venus
Will you pay me?

The Baron Docteur
I could pay you, yes.

The Venus
100 a week.

The Baron Docteur
Deal.

The Venus
New clothes and good meals.

The Baron Docteur
Whatever you want.

The Venus
My own room.

The Baron Docteur
(Rest)
Yll sleep with me.
Say "yes."

The Venus
The Baron Docteur

The Baron Docteur
Think it over. I'll stand by.

The Venus
The Baron Docteur

(Rest)

The Baron Docteur steps out of sight to let her think it over.

Enter The Mother-Showman.

She rattles a stick along the bars of the cage.

The Mother-Showman
Not gone yet?! Shit.
I guess he changed his mind.
He'll be back inny minute wanting his money
and if I dont fork it over he'll gun me down most likely Christ!
What a business this is.
9 ugly mouths to feed plus my own.
Hup Ho, Girl! Come on!
We got a crowd out there.

The Venus
(yes.)

The Mother-Showman
Theyre fresh from the pubs and I hate to say it
but the stench of liquor on their collective breaths

The Venus
(yes.)

The Baron Docteur takes The Venus from her cage.

The Mother-Showman continues her rant.

The Mother-Showman
is only matched by
the stench of yr shit in this pen, Girl! Jesus!

The Venus
(yes.)

The Mother-Showman
Jesus! *Yr an animal!*

The Venus
Yes.

The Baron Docteur
Come on then.
Lets get going.

The Venus
Yes.

The Baron Docteur
Paris! Paris! Paris! HO!

The Venus
Yes.

The Negro Resurrectionist
Scene 16:
The Intermission:

Intermission

Scene 16: Several Years from Now: In the Anatomical Theatre of Tübingen: The Dis(-re-)memberment of the Venus Hottentot, Part I

Scene 16 runs during the Intermission. House lights should come up and the audience should be encouraged to walk out of the theatre, take their intermission break, and then return.
The Baron Docteur stands at a podium.
He reads from his notebook.
The Bride-to-Be sits off to the side reading from her love letters.

The Bride-to-Be
"My love for you, My Love, is artificial
Fabricated much like this epistle."

The Baron Docteur
The height, measured after death,
was 4 feet 11 and $^1/_2$ inches.
The total weight of the body was 98 pounds *avoirdupois*.
As an aside I should say
that as to the *value* of the information that I present
to you today there can be no doubt.
Their significance
will be felt far beyond our select community. All that in mind
I understand that my yield is
long in length.
And while my finds are complete compensation

A glossary of medical terms can be found at the back of this book.

for the amount of labor expended upon them
I do invite you, Distinguished Gentlemen,
Collegues and yr Distinguished Guests,
if you need *relief*
please take yourselves uh breather in thuh lobby.
My voice will surely carry beyond these walls and if not
my finds are published. Forthcoming in *The Royal College
Journal of Anatomy*.
Merely as an aside, Gentlemen.
(Rest)

The Negro Resurrectionist
Scene 16:
Several Years from Now:
In the Anatomical Theatre of Tübingen:
The Dis(-re-)memberment of the Venus Hottentot, Part I:

The Bride-to-Be
"My Love for you, My Love, is artificial
Fabricated much like this epistle."

The Baron Docteur
The height, measured after death,
was 4 feet 11 and $1/2$ inches.
The total weight of the body was 98 pounds *avoirdupois*.
In the following notes my attention is chiefly directed
to the more perishable soft structures of the body.
The skeleton will form the subject of future examination.
(Rest)
External Characteristics:
The great amounts of subcutaneous fat were
quite surprising. On the front of the thigh for instance
fat measured 1 inch in thickness.
On the thighs reverse the measure of fat was
4 inches deep.
On the buttocks proper, rested the fatty cushion, a.k.a.
Steatopygia the details of which I'll relate in due course.
(Rest)
The Skin:
Prevaling color: Orange-brown tolerably uniform in tint
on all parts of the body save on abdomen and thighs:

2 shades darker.
(Rest)
The palms of the hands
and soles of the feet
were almost white.
(Rest)
The Face:
Remarkable for its great breadth and flatness
presenting to me resemblances to Mongolian and Simian
(previously noted by several other scholars).
The Face's Outline:
Both peculiar and characteristic
being broad in the *malar* region
contracting above the forehead but tapering suddenly
to form a narrow chin.
The great space between the eyes was 1.8: Remarkable.
The eyelids horizontal apertures were a full .95.
Irises dark brown with olive brown *conjunctiva.*
In profile the nose was nearly straight, straight on it was broad
and much depressed.
One and a half across the base and but one-half inch
one-half inch from tip to *septum.*
Nostrils, Gentlemen, were patulous,
of regular oval form: .5 in length, .3 in breadth.
Septum narium short and broad.
Aperture of mouth: 1.7 inches in width
with lips
broad and overted especially the upper one.
Chin was flat and angularish.
Ear 2.3 in its vertical diameter
the lobe quite underdeveloped.
(Rest)
The hair on the scalp was black.
Arranged in numerous separate tufts
each tuft composed of a bunch of spirally
curled hairs. Much interwoven.
The length of the tufts atop the head were from 1 inch to 1.5
becoming shorter and smaller at the scalps edge.
Several of the individual hairs when pulled out straight
were found to measure a full 7 inches.
On the scalp were several spots completely bald:

The subject when alive wore wigs which
could have produced the bare patches.
(A warning, Gentlemen, to us all.)
Eyebrows were very scanty.
Eyelashes short: .2 inch hairs.
On the *pubes* and *labia majora*
a few small scattered tufts
of crisply curled black hairs were present.
When pulled out straight these stretched out
over 3 inches long.
(Rest)
(Rest)

The Bride-to-Be

"My Love for you, My Love, is artificial
Fabricated much like this epistle.
Constructed with mans finest powrs
Will last through the days and the years and the hours."
(Rest)

The Baron Docteur

The *mammae*, situated exactly
over the fourth and fifth ribs,
were a full 6 inches apart at the inner edge of their bases.
They were soft
soft, flaccid and subpendulous:
4 inches in diameter at the base
and about the same from base to apex.
Nipple very prominent of blackish-brownish hue
and 1 inch in diameter. An areola
darker than the neighbor skin
extended around for 1 and a $^{1}/_{2}$ inches
from the nipple's center.
(Rest)
What remains of the external characters, the information,
perhaps, of greatest interest,
will be revealed toward the end of my presentation
under the head of *Generative or Reproductive Organs.*
(Rest)
The Muscular System:
(Rest)

The Bride-to-Be

"Not to a rose not to a pansy not to daffodil
Compares my Love, My Love, which will Stretch back."
(Rest)

The Baron Docteur

Presenting here, in the interest of time,
only those special points of interest.
You look, Distinguished Collegue, as if you need relief
or sleep.
Please, Sir, indulge yourself. Go take uh break.
Ive got strong lungs:
So please, if you need air, excuse yrself.
Youll hear me in the hallway.
Uh hehm:
The *Depressor anguli oris* and the *Depressor labii inferioris,*
that is, the muscles of the mouth, were both unusually
well developed, the latter
forming a distinct prominence causing
that protuberant under lip
so characteristic of the Negro tribe.
Our Anthropological scholars present will remember that
although, while during her stay with us, she picked up
uh bit of English, French and even Dutch all *patois,*
the native language of this woman is said
to have consisted entirely
of an almost uninterrupted succession
of clicks and explosives.
(Rest)
A language of *clicks*, Gentlemen.
(Rest)
The attachment of these mouth muscles was as usual.
Ear muscles, that is, *Retrahens aurem,*
were only moderately developed. They arose
by 2 slips from the base and middle of the *mastoid process*
and had the usual insertion.
The *Attollens* and *Attrahens aurem*
were injured in removing the *calvarium.*
The *Sterno-mastoid*, the muscles of the front of the neck,
and the muscles of the abdomen were distinct
in their attachments.

The former arose by a long and slender tendon, the latter
by muscular fibers from the inner end of the *clavicle*
breadth measured 1.7 inches. The *Omo-hyoid* muscle presented
a peculiarity on both sides having no origin from the *scapula*.
Its inferior extremity spread out to form a somewhat
widened attachment to the *clavicle—*
about an inch from the outer end and behind the *trapezius*.
In the muscles of the back of the neck and trunk
there was no trace of any fibers continued from the
normal *Latissimus dorsi* to represent
the *Dorso-epitrochlear* of the lower mammalia.
(Rest)
The *Levator anguli scapulae* arose from the posterior *tubercles*
of the 1st, 2nd and 4th cervical vertebrae
and had the usual insertion but with an addition:
A small slip which passed downwards
to the middle of the *Serratus magnus*.
This small slip may be an indication of the *Levator claviculae*
as noted by Dr. McWhinnie and now well known to all
    anatomists,
though the name was first recognized in human myology
by Dr. Wood. The *Splenius colli*
was inserted by a double tendon into the *transverse process*
of the 2 upper cervical vertebrae, the lower tendon
being somewhat larger. The *Cervicalis Ascendens* was
distinctly separate from the *Sacro-lumbalis*.
It arose by delicate tendons from the posterior angles
of the 1st, 2nd, 3rd and 4th ribs
which joined in a muscular belly sending off similar slips
to the *transverse process* of the 6th and 7th
hhhh cervical vertebrae.
The *Trachelo-mastoid* was divided into two portions . . .
thin delicate and membranous sprung by delicate
delicate tendons from the *transverse process* of
the 4th and 1st dorsal . . .
The *occipital* group of muscles were
all strongly developed . . .
As for the triceps, the 2 usual *humeral origins* were fused
into a single head
which reached as high as the insertion of the *Teres minor*.
Scapular origin normal.

(Rest)
The tendon of the *Extensor minimi digiti* in the right hand
divided above the annular ligament
into 2 distinct tendons
which passed under the ligament in separate grooves
and, proceeding over the *Metacarpo-phalangeal* articulation,
were reunited, and joining
with the tendon of the *Extensor communis digitorum*, formed
the tendinous expansion upon the *dorsum* of the 5th digit.
In the left hand the tendon was also split, but
the 2 divisions
(Rest)
passed through the same groove.

The Bride-to-Be

"Not to a rose not to a pansy not to daffodil
Compares my Love, My Love, which will
Stretch back and forth reach all through all Time
Deep from my heart, to pri-mordial slime."

The Baron Docteur

The *Extensor primi internodii pollicis*
was normal in its development and attachments.
(Rest)
On removing the *fascia* from the superior border
of the *Gluteus maximus* a considerable portion of the
Gluteus medius was exposed.
The condition of the *Flexor brevis digitorum pedis* presented
rather anomalous characters
it might be said to form 2 distinct muscles.
This condition interests us
because of the well-known fact that in the chimpanzee,
and all inferior Primates, a considerable portion of this muscle
always arises from the long *flexor* tendon while in man alone
the whole of it commonly takes orgin from the *Os calcis*.
(An arrangement recently described by Dr. Wood.)
The relation of the arrangements of the muscular system of Man
to that of the inferior Primates as we know
was first clearly described by Dr. Huxley
in his Hunterian Lectures
delivered at the Royal College of Surgeons earlier this year.

Unfortunately only a brief abstract has hitherto been published.
(Rest)
Her shoulders back and chest had grace.
Her charming hands . . . *uh hehm.*
Where was I?
Oh, of course:
On referring to the absolutely different characters
. . . there laid down
we find that in no case does our subject
pass over the boundary line.
(Rest)
Thank you.

He exits.

[Intermission *(continued)*:

(Historical Extract. Musical: The Song of Jack Higgenbottom)

Wonder #7 sings a song.

Wonder #7
A song on behalf of myself and The Hottentot Venus, to the
    Ladies of New York:
"Fair Ladies, Ive saild, in obedience to you
from New York, since the last Masquerade, to Peru.
There, to guard gainst all possible scandal tonight
I turnd Priest and have conjurd my Black-a-moor white.
A strange Metamorphosis!—who that had seen us
tother night, would take this for *The Hottentot Venus.*
Or me for poor Jack? Now Im Priest of the Sun
and she, a queer kind of Peruvian Nun.
Though in this our Novitiate, we *preach* but so, so
youll grant that at least we *appear* comme il faut.
In pure Virgin robes, full of fears and alarms
how demurely she veils her protuberant charms!
Thus oft, to atone for absurdities past
Tom Foll turns a Methodist Preacher at last.
Yet the *Critics* not *we* were to blame—for od rot em
there was nothing but innocent fun *at the bottom!*"

Wonder #7 exits.**]**
End of Intermission.

Scene 15: Counting Down

The Negro Resurrectionist
31
30
29
28
27
26
25
24
23
22
21
20
19
18
17
16
15
14
(Rest)
Scene 14:

Scene 14: In the Orbital Path of the Baron Docteur

The lovers in bed.

The Baron Docteur
Quatorze
Treize
Douze
Onze
Dix
Neuf
Huit
Sept
Six
Cinq
Quatre
Trois
Deux
Un
(Rest)
Its dark in here. Spooky.
Lets have light.

The Venus
Keep it dark.
Are yr eyes closed?

The Baron Docteur
Theyre closed.
Hurry up. Im eager.

The Negro Resurrectionist
Scene #14:
In the Orbital Path of the Baron Docteur:

Venus
Voilà. Open yr eyes.

The Baron Docteur
The Venus

The Baron Docteur
Too dark to see.
Lie here beside me, Sweetheart.
Mmmm. Thats good.

The Venus
Love me?

The Baron Docteur
I do.
Ah, this is the life.

> He recites a poem.

The Baron Docteur
"My love for you is artificial
Fabricated much like this epistle.
Its crafted with my finest powers
To last through the days and the weeks and the hours."
(Rest)
I made it up myself.
Just this morning.
You like it?

The Venus
I love it.

The Baron Docteur and The Venus
Mmmmmmmmm.

The Venus
The Baron Docteur

(Rest)

The Baron Docteur
You know what I want more than anything?

The Venus
Me.
Lets have some love.

The Baron Docteur
After you. Guess what I want.

The Venus
More me.
Kiss?

The Baron Docteur
Im an everyday anatomist.
One in a crowd of millions.

The Venus
Another kiss.
Mmmm thats good.
Sweetheart, lie back down.

The Baron Docteur
You were just yrself and crowds came running.
I was fascinated and a little envious but just a little.
A doctor cant just be himself
no onell pay a cent for that.
Imagine me just being me.

The Venus
Hahahahahahaha.

The Baron Docteur
What a strange laugh.

The Venus
Lie back down.
Hold me close to you. Its cold.
Love me?

The Baron Docteur
I do.

The Venus
The Baron Docteur
The Venus

(Rest)

The Baron Docteur
Most great minds discover something.
Ive had ideas for things but.
My ideas r—
(You wouldnt understand em anyway.)

The Venus
Touch me
down here.

The Baron Docteur
In you, Sweetheart, Ive met my opposite-exact.
Now if I could only match you.

The Venus
That feels good.
Now touch me here.

The Baron Docteur
Crowds of people screamd yr name!
    "Venus Hottentot!!"
You were a sensation! I wouldnt mind a bit of that.
Known. Like you!
Only, of course, in my specific circle.

The Venus
You could be whatshisname: Columbus.

The Baron Docteur
Thats been done.

The Venus
Columbus II?

The Baron Docteur
Dont laugh at me.
(Rest)

The Venus
The Baron Docteur
The Venus

(Rest)

The Baron Docteur
Here. Yr favorite: Chockluts. Have some.

     The Baron Docteur turns his back to her.

The Venus
Petits Coeurs
Rhum Caramel
Pharaon
Bouchon Fraise
Escargot Lait
Enfant de Bruxelles.
(Rest)
Do you think I look like
one of these little chocolate brussels infants?

The Baron Docteur
You cant stay here forever you know.

The Venus
Capezzoli di Venere.
The nipples of Venus. Mmmmm. My favorite.

The Baron Docteur
Ive got a wife. Youve got a homeland and a family back there.

The Venus
I dont wanna go back inny more.
I like yr company too much.
Besides, it was a shitty life.

A glossary of chocolate can be found at the back of this book.

(Rest)
Whatre you doing?

The Baron Docteur
Nothing.

The Venus
Lemmie see.

The Baron Docteur
Dont look! Dont look at me.
Look off
somewhere.
Eat yr chockluts
eat em slow
thats it.
Touch yrself.
Good.
Good.

> He's masturbating. He has his back to her. He sneaks little
> looks at her over his shoulder. He cums.

The Venus
Whyd you do that?

The Baron Docteur
Im polite.
(Rest)

The Venus
Love me?

The Baron Docteur
Do I ever.

The Venus
More than yr wife?

The Baron Docteur
More than my life.

And my wife.
She and I are childless you know.

The Venus
I know.
These are yummy.
(Rest)
Wear this uhround yr neck and never take it off.
Its uh good luck feather. Uh sort of amulet.
It might help.

The Baron Docteur
It smells of you.

The Venus
Love me?

The Baron Docteur
Yes.
You dont want to go home?

The Venus
Not inny more.
(Rest)
Love me?

The Baron Docteur
I do.

The Venus
Lie down.
And kiss me.
Here.
And here.
And here.
And here.
And here, you missed a spot,
Dearheart.

The Baron Docteur
Dearheart.

The Venus
You could discover *me*.

The Baron Docteur
The Venus
The Baron Docteur

(Rest)

The Baron Docteur
The Venus
The Baron Docteur

(Rest)

The Baron Docteur
I love you, Girl.

The Venus
Lights out.

Scene 13: Footnote #7

The Negro Resurrectionist reads from
The Baron Docteur's notebook.

The Negro Resurrectionist
Footnote #7:
Historical Extract. Category: Medical.
(Rest)
A DETAILED PHYSICAL DESCRIPTION OF THE
SO-CALLED VENUS HOTTENTOT:
(Rest)
"Her hair was black and wooly, much like that of the common
Negro, the slits of the eyes horizontal as in Mongols, not
oblique; the brows straight, wide apart and very much flat-
tened close to the top of the nose, but jutting out at the tem-
ple above the cheekbones; her eyes were dark and lively; her
lips blackish, terribly thick; her complexion very dark."
(Rest)
"Her ears were much like those found in monkeys: Small, weakly
formed at the *tragus*, and vanishing behind almost completely."
(Rest)
"Her breasts she usually lifted and tightened beneath the
middle part of her dress, but, left free, they hung bulkily and
terminated obliquely in a blackish areola about 1 and $1/2$ inches in diameter pitted with radiating wrinkles, near the center
of what was a nipple so flattened and obliterated as to be barely
visible: The color of her skin was on the whole a yellowish
brown, almost as dark as her face."
(Rest)
"Her movements had rapidity and came unexpected calling
to mind well, with all respect to her, the movements of a mon-

key. Above all, she had a way of pushing out her lips just like the monkeys do. Her personality was sprightly, her memory good. She spoke low Dutch, tolerably good English—the men at the Academy and I tried to teach her French. She danced after the fashion of her own country and played with a fairly good ear upon a little instrument she called a Jew's Harp."
(Rest)
"She had no body hair apart from a few short flecks of wool like that on her head, scattered about her pubic parts."
(Rest)
"The wonders of her lower regions, will be fleshed out in greater detail at a later date."
(Rest)
"This information was gleaned, as has been said, upon the first and subsequent examinations which were performed in the office of her personal physician. As stated for the record, she submitted to these examinations as willingly as a patient submits to his doctors eyes and hands."
(Rest)
Scene #12:

Scene 12: Love Iduhnt What/She Used to Be

> The Venus stands alone. She's dressed
> in a beautiful dress and looks fabulous.
> The Chorus of the 8 Anatomists wanders in one by one.
> They get to work.
> The Baron Docteur wanders in. He watches.
> He wears his feather amulet.

Anatomist #8
"The book is on the table!"

The Venus
*Le livre est
sur la table!*

Anatomist #8
"The book is on the floor!"

The Venus
*Le livre est
par terre!*

Anatomist #8
"And now the book is on my shoulder!"

The Venus
*Et maintenant, le livre est
sur mon épaule!*

Anatomist #8
"And now the book is on my head!"

The Venus
Et maintenant, le livre est
sur ma tête!

> The Chorus of the 8 Anatomists applauds most respectfully.

Anatomist #8
Thats excellent! And shes only been here
what, Sir, 6 months?

The Baron Docteur
6 months thats right.

Anatomist #8
Throws all of those throw-back theories back in the lake, I'd say.
Throw em back in the lake!

The Baron Docteur
Not entirely, Gentlemen.
We study a people as a group
and dont throw away our years of labor
because of one most glorious exception.

The Chorus of the 8 Anatomists
Hahahahahahahahahaha.

> The Anatomists and The Baron Docteur laugh
> good-naturedly. The Venus joins in.
> While they laugh a new Anatomist wanders onstage. He is
> The Baron Docteur's Grade-School Chum. He surreptitiously
> hands The Baron Docteur a letter and wanders off.

The Baron Docteur
Enough play, Gentlemen!
Lets get to work!

> The Venus denudes. Perhaps 2 of the female Anatomists
> assist her. She is lightly clothed in a sheer fabric.

The Baron Docteur
We'll start with simple figure drawing.

An important skill for any promising Anatomist.
(Rest)
Sweetheart, stand here where the light is perfect on you.
Just relax.
Only doctors here.
Thats beautiful.
(Rest)
Alright, Gentlemen! Pose #1.

> The Venus stands in profile as they sketch her.
> The Baron Docteur stands apart and reads his letter.

The Baron Docteur
("Dear Sir:
I am a friend of yrs from way back.
Im sure you remember at least my face
we went to school together. How interesting
that we're both in the doctoring business.
But no time for reminiscing, old friend,
I must cut straight to the point:
In yr liason with that Negress, Sir, you disgrace yrself.
Not to mention the pain yr causing yr sweet lovely wife.
A year in her bed is plenty, Sir. Surely yve tired of her
    heathen charms by now.
Send the Thing back where she came from
and return yrself to the bosom of yr senses.
Im speaking plain because as an old friend Ive
made it my responsiblilty to bring you back.
Sincerly yrs,
A Grade-School Chum.")
(Rest)
(Rest)
Gentlemen!
On to pose #2!
(Rest)
Sweetheart, reverse profile, if you please.

> The Venus stands in reverse profile.
> The Chorus of the 8 Anatomists draws busily.
> The Baron Docteur stands apart.

The Baron Docteur
"Sincerely yrs, A Grade-School Chum."
(Rest)
(Rest)
"I'm sure you remember at least my face."
(Rest)
(Rest)
"A Grade-School Chum."
Ah, ridiculous!
"A Grade-School Chum." Ha!
Just some busy eager beaver
trying to beat my time, I'll bet.
(Rest)
(Rest)

The Venus
The Baron Docteur
The Venus
The Baron Docteur

(Rest)

The Venus
Love me?

The Baron Docteur
How couldnt I?
Yr lovelier than ever.

The Venus
The Baron Docteur

(Rest)
(Rest)

The Baron Docteur
Gentlemen!
Time to practice Measurements!

> The Chorus of the 8 Anatomists measures The Venus.
> The Baron Docteur stands apart.

The Baron Docteur
From thuh *vertex* to thuh chin:

The Chorus of the 8 Anatomists
8.0 inches.

The Baron Docteur
Vertex to
the top of shoulder in inches:

The Chorus of the 8 Anatomists
9.0.

The Baron Docteur
To thuh upper part of thuh *sternum*:

The Chorus of the 8 Anatomists
10.5.

The Baron Docteur
To thuh *formal cartilages tip*:

The Chorus of the 8 Anatomists
16.3.

The Baron Docteur
To the *umbilicus*:

The Chorus of the 8 Anatomists
To the *umbilicus*:
23.5.

The Baron Docteur
To the *perineum*:

The Chorus of the 8 Anatomists
To the *perineum*:
30.0.

The Baron Docteur
To the middle fingers tip
the arm being placed by the side:

The Chorus of the 8 Anatomists
32.2.

The Baron Docteur
To the middle fingers tip
the arm being extended from the side:

The Chorus of the 8 Anatomists
32.1.

Again, The Grade-School Chum wanders in and surreptitiously
hands The Baron Docteur another letter. This time
The Grade-School Chum joins the group of measurers.

The Baron Docteur
To the middle fingers tip
the arm being extended towards the viewer
full front:

The Chorus of the 8 Anatomists
32.1.

The Baron Docteur
To the lower edge
of the *patella*:

The Chorus of the 8 Anatomists
41.3.

The Baron Docteur
To the sole of the foot:

The Chorus of the 8 Anatomists
To the sole of the foot:
55.9.
(Rest)

The Baron Docteur
("Dear Sir:
Perhaps my first letter went unnoticed,
one scrap of paper

one among the several thousands littering yr desk and yr hot
   bed.")
(Rest)
Transverse breadth of the head:

The Chorus of the 8 Anatomists
5.2.

The Baron Docteur
Transverse breadth of the shoulders:

The Chorus of the 8 Anatomists
12.0.

The Baron Docteur
Transverse breadth, *thorax* at the lower part:

The Chorus of the 8 Anatomists
8.4.

The Baron Docteur
Thorax at *axilla*:

The Chorus of the 8 Anatomists
8.7.

The Baron Docteur
("Another year has passed since I first wrote.
And although youve not married yr pet Hottentot
and play a good part with yr dear wife . . .")
(Rest)
Pelvis at the crest of the ilium:

The Chorus of the 8 Anatomists
8.6.

The Baron Docteur
Pelvis at the great *trochanters*:

The Chorus of the 8 Anatomists
Pelvis at the great *trochanters*:
11.0.
(Rest)

The Baron Docteur
Length of the *humerus*:

The Chorus of the 8 Anatomists
10.0.

The Baron Docteur
Of the *radius*:

The Chorus of the 8 Anatomists
7.3.

The Baron Docteur
Of the *ulna*:

The Chorus of the 8 Anatomists
7.9.

The Baron Docteur
Of the *femur*:

The Chorus of the 8 Anatomists
Length of the *femur*:
14.5.

The Baron Docteur
Of the *tibia*:

The Chorus of the 8 Anatomists
11.3.

The Baron Docteur
((“I'd like to think its my note thats moved you to return
    home although
you reek of Hottentot-amour, Sir, and as a collegue its my
    duty to speak plain, Sir:
we all smell it!”))
(Rest)
(Rest)

       The Chorus of the 8 Anatomists sniffs the air.

The Baron Docteur
(Rest)
Of the spine from the upper border of the *atlas*
to the tip of the *coccyx*:

The Chorus of the 8 Anatomists
23.8.

The Baron Docteur
The Baron Docteur
The Baron Docteur
The Baron Docteur

> The Baron Docteur is lost in thought.
> The Chorus of the 8 Anatomists waits patiently for him
> to resume, then, turning their backs to The Venus,
> they steal looks over their shoulders at her and jerk off
> (much like The Baron Docteur did in Scene 14).

The Baron Docteur
(Rest)
Of the spine to the last lumbar vertebra:

The Chorus of the 8 Anatomists
19.2.

The Baron Docteur
(Rest)
Circumference of the chest at the lower margin
of the 6th rib:

The Chorus of the 8 Anatomists
27.5.

The Baron Docteur
(Rest)
Span of the arms when extended:
Pull em all the way out, Gentlemen!

The Chorus of the 8 Anatomists
Span of the arms
all the way out:
58.9.

The Grade-School Chum
The measurements of her limb-bones
will of course
be corrected
after maceration, Sir?

The Baron Docteur
The Grade-School Chum

The Venus
"Maceration?"

The Negro Resurrectionist
Footnote #8:
Definition: Medical: *Maceration*:
(Rest)
"A process performed on the subject after the subjects death.
The subjects body parts are soaked in a chemical solution to
separate the flesh from the bones so that the bones may be
measured with greater accuracy."
(Rest)

The Baron Docteur
Thats enough for now.
Gentlemen:
Thats plenty for today and Im sure our lovely subjects
all exhausted.
Put yr hands together, Sirs.
Show The Venus yr appreciation.

They applaud politely.

The Negro Resurrectionist
Scene 11:
From "For the Love of the Venus." Act II, Scene 12:

Scene 11: "For the Love of the Venus." Act II, Scene 12

        The Baron Docteur's chair is empty. The Negro
    Resurrectionist takes a seat and watches halfheartedly.

The Bride-to-Be
He sez he loves a Hottentot.

The Mother
Dont snuffle.

The Bride-to-Be
A *Hottentot!*

The Mother
Blow yr nose.

The Bride-to-Be
Hottentot Venus!

The Mother
Wipe yr eyes.
My Sons gone wild
but I have a plan.
Listen up!
(Rest)
His head has turned from yr bright sun.
He roams in thuh dark.
Let me speak plain:
He dudhnt love you inny more.

The Bride-to-Be
Aaah me!

The Mother

[Uh multitude of responses are available.
Thuh antiquity response would be thuh Asp.
Get yrself uh poison-snake. Clasp it tuh yr bosom.
On thuh left side. Let it fill yr heart with death.
Cleopatra. Very moving. Old hat now though.
Thuh classical response would be tuh hang yrself.
Phaedra did that.
Elizabethan response would be tuh drown yrself.
A la little wassername.

The Bride-to-Be

Ophelia.

The Mother

Good girl.
They also drank poison. Fell on their swords.
In modern dress they slit their wrists.
Fill their pockets with rocks.
Jump from bridges.
Infront of trains.
Sleeping pills. Take one or two too many. Thatll do it.
Hunger strike: Turn yr face tuh thuh wall dont eat for weeks.
Thats like pining. But more dramatic.
To simply waste uhway—]
But none of that.
I have uh plan.
Get this:
Our young man wants uh Hottentot tuh love.
Uh Hottentot yr not, my dear.
But with some skill you can pretend.

The Bride-to-Be

Pretend?

The Mother

Lets get to work.
I'll get that Uncle on our side.
We'll get you up, make you look wild
Get you up like a Hottentot.

The Bride-to-Be
Like a Hottentot?

The Mother
Bring my Son to his knees.
Lets get to work.

The Bride-to-Be
Lets get to work.

Curtain.
The Chorus applauds.

Scene 10: Footnote #9

The Negro Resurrectionist reads from
The Baron Docteur's notebook.

The Negro Resurrectionist
(Rest)
Footnote #9:
Historical Extract. Category: Medical.
(Rest)
"The female Hottentot under my care has the usual falling off
of appearance common in women of 30 years old. Her *mammae* are flaccid and elongated. While her *glutei* muscles along
with their coverings, the 2 prominent peculiar hemispherical
cushions of fat, are quite remarkable, more remarkable still are
the long appendages which hang down from her *pudendum!*"

The Baron Docteur snatches his notebook from
The Negro Resurrectionist's hands.

The Baron Docteur
The Negro Resurrectionist

The Negro Resurrectionist
Scene #9:
Her Charming Hands/
An Anatomical Columbus:

Scene 9: Her Charming Hands/An Anatomical Columbus

> The Venus sits in the chair
> wrapped up to her chin in a large cloth.
> The Baron Docteur stands above her wielding a shiny and
> sharp pair of scissors. He is giving her a haircut.

The Baron Docteur
Hold still.
There now.
Open yr eyes and take a look.

The Venus
Uh uhnn.

The Baron Docteur
Its almost perfect.

The Venus
Im nervous.
I could be bald.

The Baron Docteur
Ive got the steadiest hands in the business.
Dearheart. Look.

The Venus
Mmm.
Not bad.
A little uneven on the left.
Just there.

> He evens out her haircut.

The Baron Docteur
Did yr dresses come today?

The Venus
They did.

The Baron Docteur
Wear the yellow one tonight.

The Venus
We're having company?

The Baron Docteur
No.
Tonights dinner is just you and me.

The Venus
Its always only you and me.
You and me this room that table.
We dont go out.
No one visits.
You dont want me seen.

The Baron Docteur
Yr seen enough at the Academy.

The Venus
That dont count.

The Baron Docteur
We go for rides.

The Venus
In a closed coach!

The Baron Docteur
Ok Ok I confess:
I wanna keep my Sweets
all to myself.
Im very greedy.
(Rest)
Take another look.

The Venus
Looks alright.
Love me?

The Baron Docteur
Mmm.

The Venus
The Baron Docteur

(Rest)

The Baron Docteur
Ok, up up!
Ive got some work to do
before we eat.

The Venus
Put yr hand here.

The Baron Docteur
Yr warm.

The Venus
Yes.

The Baron Docteur
Upset stomach? I'll fix you something.
You eat too many chockluts you know.
I give em to you by the truckload but
you dont have to eat them all.
Practice some restraint.
Drink this.

The Venus
Put yr hand here, Sweetheart.

The Baron Docteur
Drink this first.

The Venus
No. Feel me.

The Baron Docteur
Fine.

The Venus
The Baron Docteur
The Venus
The Baron Docteur

(Rest)

The Baron Docteur
What am I feeling?

The Venus
Guess.

The Venus
The Baron Docteur
The Venus
The Baron Docteur

                                                    She's pregnant.

(Rest)

The Baron Docteur
God. Is there anything we can do about it.
Ive a wife. A career.
A reputation. Is there anything
we can do about it we together in
the privacy of my office.
Ive got various equipments in here
we could figure something out.

The Venus
The Venus
The Venus

The Venus
Where I come from
its cause for celebration.

The Baron Docteur
A simple yes or no will do, Girl.
(Rest)

The Venus
Yes.

The Baron Docteur
Fine.
We'll take care of it this evening.
After dinner.
Is that alright?

The Venus
Yes thats fine.

The Baron Docteur
Fine.

The Venus
The Baron Docteur

(Rest)

She exits.

The Baron Docteur
The Baron Docteur

(Rest)

The Grade-School Chum appears as if out of thin air.

The Grade-School Chum
The Baron Docteur
The Grade-School Chum
The Baron Docteur

The Grade-School Chum
The door was wide open.
I walked right in.

You 2 should keep yr voices down.
Everyone kin hear yr business.
(Rest)
Dont you recognize me?

The Baron Docteur
Cant say I do.

The Grade-School Chum
We went to school together.
Remember?
(Rest)

The Baron Docteur
The Grade-School Chum

(Rest)

The Baron Docteur
Vaguely.

The Grade-School Chum
I was the one who ripped the wings off the flies.
We were like brothers.
Hug me!

The Baron Docteur
Beat it.

The Grade-School Chum
Whats that thing around yr neck.

The Baron Docteur
None of yr business.

The Grade-School Chum
Get rid of her.
Shes not yr type.

The Baron Docteur
Good evening, Sir.
I'll show you out.

The Grade-School Chum
Yr wifes distraught.

The Baron Docteur
No she is not!

The Grade-School Chum
Yr reputation is in shambles.

The Baron Docteur
My discoveriesll right that.

The Grade-School Chum
You better dissect her soon, Old Friend,
the Academy wont wait for ever.

The Baron Docteur
I'll dissect her soon enough!

The Grade-School Chum
Ive come as a friend.
Giving friendly advice.

The Baron Docteur
Friend.
I am to her a mere
Anatomical Columbus.
Lemmie read you a little
of what Ive written so far.
Where to begin? *Uh hehm*

He reads from his notebook.

(("... the vast protuberance of her buttocks...
The somewhat brutish appearance of her face."))

The Grade-School Chum
So get rid of her!
Break with her!
Kick her out on her fat ass!

The Baron Docteur
But, I
I love her.
I love her!!

Scene 8: "For the Love of the Venus." Act III, Scene 9

The Negro Resurrectionist is the only audience.
The Uncle presents The Bride-to-Be disguised as
The Hottentot Venus.

The Uncle
Presenting:
Presenting:
Young Man, to you for love alone
the Wild Thing of yr hearts desire:
From the darkest jungles may I present: "The Hottentot Venus!"

The Young Man
The Hottentot Venus
The Young Man
The Hottentot Venus

(Rest)

The Father
Young Man, say something.

The Young Man
Good God good God.
She is so odd.
Love?
Youre Love?

The Hottentot Venus
The Young Man
The Hottentot Venus
The Young Man

132

(Rest)

The Young Man
She doesnt speak?

The Uncle
Not many words we understand.
Her hometown lingos uh strange one
Therefore, Hottentot Venus, darling,
allow me to interpret.
(Rest)
Hottentot Venus, you speak first.
(Rest)

| **The Uncle** | They click and cluck at each other. |
| **The Hottentot Venus** | |

(Rest)

The Uncle
Young Man, she says shes Love.

The Young Man
Whisper, ask her, if shes wild.

| **The Uncle** | More clicking. More clucking. |
| **The Hottentot Venus** | |

(Rest)

The Uncle
She sez she comes from far uhway where its quite hot.
She sez shes pure bred Hottentot.
She sez if Wilds your desire
she comes from The Wilds and she carries them behind her.
[Wild is her back-ground her fundament so to speak
and although shes grown accustomed to our civil ways
she still holds The Wilds within her
behind, inside, infront
which is to say, that all yr days
with her will be a lively lovely bliss.]

The Young Man
Let me look at her!

The Uncle
Circle around
get all her angles.

>   The Young Man orbits briefly.

The Young Man
The Hottentot Venus
The Young Man

>   He stares hard at her.
>   The Young Man and The Hottentot Venus stand in tableau.

The Negro Resurrectionist
"The height, measured after death,
was 4 feet 11 and $^1/_2$ inches.
The total weight of the body was 98 pounds *avoirdupois* . . .
The great amounts of subcutaneous fat were
quite surprising."
(Rest)
Scene #7:

Scene 7: She'll Make a Splendid Corpse

Bright sunshine.
The Venus in her bedroom daydreaming. She wears a wig.

The Venus

He spends all his time with me because he loves me.
He hardly visits her at all.
She may be his wife all right but shes all dried up.
He is not thuh most thrilling lay Ive had
but his gold makes up thuh difference and hhhh
I love him.
He will leave that wife for good and we'll get married
(we better or I'll make a scene) oh, we'll get married.
And we will lie in bed and make love all day long.
Hahahaha.
We'll set tongues wagging for the rest of the century.
The Docteur will introduce me to Napoléon himself: Oh,
yes yr Royal Highness the Negro question does keep me
awake at night oh yes it does.
Servant girl! Do this and that!
When Im Mistress I'll be a tough cookie.
I'll rule the house with an iron fist and have the most
    fabulous parties.
Society will seek me out: Wheres Venus? Right here!
Hhhhh. I need a new wig.
Every afternoon I'll take a 3 hour bath. In hot rosewater.
After my bath theyll pat me down.
Theyll rub my body with the most expensive oils
perfume my big buttocks and sprinkle them with gold dust!

The Baron Docteur enters and watches her.
She does not see him.

The Venus
Come here quick, slave and attend me!
Fetch my sweets! Fix my hair!
Do this do that do this do that!
Hahahahahahah! Mmmmmmm.

The Baron Docteur
What are you doing?

The Venus
Oh.
Im sunning myself.

The Baron Docteur
Then you should have a parasol.

The Venus
No thanks.
Kiss me.

The Baron Docteur
Little Hotsey-Totsey.

The Venus
Come to bed.

The Baron Docteur
Its the middle of the day.

The Venus
So?

The Baron Docteur
Mmmm.

The Venus
The Baron Docteur

The Venus
I dont think I wanna go to yr Academy inny more.

The Baron Docteur
Dont be silly.
They all love you there.
And yr French is brilliant.
Its only been 2 years and yr sounding like a native.
Yr a linguistic genius!
Everybody agrees.

The Venus
They touch me sometimes.
When yr not looking.

The Baron Docteur
How could they not?
Touching you is—well, its their job.

The Venus
Theyre lascivious.

The Baron Docteur
Jesus.
Dont be hyperbolic.

The Venus
You seem half there.
Love me?
(Rest)

The Baron Docteur
The Venus

(Rest)

The Baron Docteur
Im here arent I?

The Venus
I'll wake up one day youll be gone.

The Baron Docteur
Wrong.

Im here to stay.
Things are just a little off at work thats all.

The Venus
Touch me
down here.

The Baron Docteur
What is it?

The Venus
The Baron Docteur

She's pregnant again.

(Rest)

The Baron Docteur
Can we do anything? Oh God.

The Venus
Oh God.

The Baron Docteur
A simple yes or no will do.

The Venus
Im not feeling very well.
Its hot in here.
Love me?

The Baron Docteur
A simple yes or no will do, Girl!

The Venus
Yes.
Yes.

The Baron Docteur
Good. Now get some sleep.

The Venus
The Baron Docteur
The Venus
The Baron Docteur

(Rest)

The Venus
Whats "maceration."

The Baron Docteur
Huh?

The Venus
"Maceration."

The Baron Docteur
Whyd you ask?

The Venus
They always say:
"The measurementsll be corrected after
'maceration.'" Whats it mean?

The Baron Docteur
"Macerations" French for "lunch."
"After lunch" we also say.
(Rest)
Yr my true Love.
Now get some sleep.

> They sleep.
> Enter The Grade-School Chum, as if in a dream.
> The Baron Docteur wakes up with a start.

The Grade-School Chum
Ready now:
Cough.

The Baron Docteur
Uhh!

The Grade-School Chum
Turn yr head.
Cough uhgain.

The Baron Docteur
Uhh!
Yr not my regular physician.

The Grade-School Chum
Nope.
Say "Aaaah."

The Baron Docteur
"Aaaah."

The Grade-School Chum
Bigger.

The Baron Docteur
"Aaaaaaah?"
(Rest)
Shes my True Love.
She'd make uh splendid wife.

The Grade-School Chum
Yr sick.

The Baron Docteur
Thatsright.

The Grade-School Chum
Whatwith?

The Baron Docteur
True Love.

The Grade-School Chum
Yr reputation is in shambles.

The Baron Docteur
So?

The Grade-School Chum
Yr wifes distraught.

The Baron Docteur
Oh, she is not!

The Grade-School Chum
Whats so great about the black girl tell me.

The Baron Docteur
Get lost.

The Grade-School Chum
Yr still childless with the Mrs. arent you.

The Baron Docteur
Beat it.

The Grade-School Chum
And a laughing stock of the Academy to boot.
Whats that uhround yr neck?

The Baron Docteur
Uh charm. For luck. Get lost.

The Grade-School Chum
Here: A pill. Take it. Doctors orders.
Itll clear yr head.
Go on. Doctors orders.
Take it now.
Wash it down.
Aaaah?

The Baron Docteur
Aaah.

> The Grade-School Chum tosses a pill in
> The Baron Docteur's mouth and he swallows it down.

The Grade-School Chum
Yr breath is off. Smells like—woah: Fuck.
I wouldnt wear that. Looks like bad luck.

The Baron Docteur
You think?

The Grade-School Chum
I do. Lets take it off.
Im doing you a favor, Man:
Im packing yr bags and Im bringing you with me.

The Baron Docteur
Do I have a choice?

The Grade-School Chum
Sure.
But you know, of course,
yr not the only Doc
whos got hisself uh Hottentot.

The Baron Docteur
The Grade-School Chum

(Rest)

The Grade-School Chum
The Baron Docteur

(Rest)
(Rest)

The Baron Docteur
Speak plainly, Friend.

The Grade-School Chum
Some chap in Germany or somethin
got his hands on one.
He performed the autopsy today.
Word is he'll publish inny minute.

The Baron Docteur
He'll beat me to the punch!

The Grade-School Chum
What do you care
yr in Luv.

The Baron Docteur
The Grade-School Chum

The Baron Docteur
Shes not feeling so well.
Said so herself.

The Grade-School Chum
She'll probably outlive us all.

The Baron Docteur
Shes—
Shes got the clap.

The Grade-School Chum
The clap?
From you?

The Baron Docteur
Perhaps.
(Rest)
It makes my work with her
indecent somehow.

The Grade-School Chum
"Indecency!"
We could clap her into jail for that.

The Baron Docteur
We could?

The Grade-School Chum
Its up to you of course.
(Rest)
Remember who you are, Sir,
and make the right decision.
Say yes and we'll have her gone by morning.

The Baron Docteur
There must be some other solution.

The Grade-School Chum
We'll clap her into jail.
And if her clap runs its course, well,
thats fate, Friend.

The Baron Docteur
Oh God.

The Grade-School Chum
A simple yes or no will do, Doctor.
Come on.

The Baron Docteur
Such a lovely creature in her way.
She has a grace—

The Grade-School Chum
Come on.
Say yes.
Before she wakes.

The Baron Docteur
Her charming hands—

The Grade-School Chum
Shes just a 2-bit sideshow freak.

The Baron Docteur
She would have made uh splendid wife.

The Grade-School Chum
Oh, please.
She'll make uh splendid corpse.

> The Grade-School Chum exits leading
> The Baron Docteur by the hand.
> The Venus wakes up with a start. She is alone.

The Venus
The Venus
The Venus
The Venus

(Rest)

The Venus
Is it uh little hot in here
or is it just me?

(Rest)

The Venus
The Venus
The Venus
The Venus

> A knot of Spectators gathers around her.

The Chorus of the Spectators
Lookie-Lookie-Lookie-Lookie
Hubba-Hubba-Hubba-Hubba
Lookie-Lookie-Lookie-Lookie
Hubba-Hubba-Hubba-Hubba.
(Rest)

The Chorus of the Spectators
The Venus
The Chorus of the Spectators

(Rest)

> The Chorus of the Spectators bursts into a riot.
> The Venus flees.

The Negro Resurrectionist
Order!
Order!
Order!
Order!

Suddenly The Venus is again imprisoned.
Not caged but chained like a dog in the yard.
The Negro Resurrectionist seats himself beside her.
He is her guard.

The Venus
The Negro Resurrectionist
The Venus
The Negro Resurrectionist

The Grade-School Chum
Indecency?
Clap her into jail for that!

The Baron Docteur
Clap her into jail for that?

The Chorus of the Spectators applauds.

Scene 6: Some Years Later in Tübingen (Reprise)

The Chorus of the Spectators applauds.
The Baron Docteur reads from his notebook.

The Baron Docteur
Uh hehm
(Rest)
"In regards to the formation of her buttocks
we make the following remarks:
The fatty cushion, a.k.a.
Steatopygia was 9 inches deep. Her buttocks—"
Uh hehm.

The Negro Resurrectionist
Scene #6:
Several Years Later, at a Conference in Tübingen:
The Dis(-re-)memberment of the Venus Hottentot, Part II:

The Baron Docteur
"Her buttocks had nearly
nearly the usual origin and insertion
but the muscular fibers were surprisingly thin and flabby
and very badly developed thus showing that
the protuberance of the buttocks
so peculiar to the Bushman race
is not the result of any muscular development but rather
totally dependent
on the accumulation of fat."
(Rest)

The Venus is chained. The Negro Ressurectionist stands watch.

The Venus
You ever Love?

The Negro Resurrectionist
Naw.

The Venus
No?

The Negro Resurrectionist
Nope.

The Venus
Ever been loved?

The Negro Resurrectionist
Uh uhnnn.
(Rest)   He gives her a red heart box
Chockluts. Here.   of chocolates.
Theyre not from me.
Theyre from a man who sez he knew you when.
Doctor I think he sed.

The Venus
"Doctor?"

The Negro Resurrectionist
Maybe once when you were sick?

(Rest)

The Baron Docteur continues with great difficulty.

The Baron Docteur
Oh God my mind was wandering
Where was I?
Uh hehm:
"While the uterus had the ordinary form of that organ in a
once or twice impregnated female,

the external characters,
especially of the reproductive organs,
form, in this view, the centerpiece of Study.
(Rest)
The *labia majora* were small.
The clitoris sized moderate to large
and had a well-developed *prepuce*
all situated far more conspicuously
than in the European female.
Her most remarkable feature
were the long appendages
which hung down from her *pudendum.*
They resembled 2 thongs
each about the thickness of a cedar-wood pencil
exactly like strips of sheepskin slightly twisted
and apparently vascular.
On separating her *labia* I found these *appendages*
to be the *nymphae* elongated.
I took up her appendages
and led the right one round her right side
above her gluteal projection, similarly
I led her left appendage round her left side
and their ends *met at her spine.*
(Rest)
There was no trace of hymen.
(Rest)
(Rest)
The remarkable development of the *labia minora*
which heretofore is so general a characteristic of
the Hottentot or Bushman race
was so sufficiently well marked that it well distinguished itself
from those of any of the ordinary varieties of the human species.
Again, their difference was so marked
their formation so distinguished
that they formed this studies centerpiece.
This author recommends further examination of said formation."
(Rest)
Thank you.

He stands there holding his notebook and hanging his head.

Scene 5: Who Is She to Me?

The Venus sleeps. The Negro Resurrectionist stands watch.

The Grade-School Chum
You watch The Venus Hottentot?

The Negro Resurrectionist
Im her Watchman, thats right.
And I'll put her safely in the ground when she dies too.
Whats that to you?

The Grade-School Chum
I recognize you, Man
I know you from way back.
Youve got a memorable face.

The Negro Resurrectionist
So what.

The Grade-School Chum
You used to unearth bodies
for my postmortem class.
An illegal craft as I remember.

The Negro Resurrectionist
I quit that line years ago.

The Grade-School Chum
Once a *digger* always one.

The Negro Resurrectionist
Get to the point.

The Grade-School Chum
A friend of mine in the medical profession
is very interested in the body of yr ward.
After she "goes on."
For scientific analysis only of course.

The Negro Resurrectionist
No thank you.

The Grade-School Chum
I'll have to call the cops on you.
Theyll lock you up.

The Negro Resurrectionist
I quit that buisiness!

The Grade-School Chum
Yd be surprised at how
the legal system works.
(Rest)
Shes gonna kick it inny minute.
We'll pay you for yr trouble.
Its not for me but for a friend.
He doesnt got the balls to ask.

> The Grade-School Chum knees
> The Negro Resurrectionist in the balls.

The Grade-School Chum
We'll pay you well. In gold.
Say yes.

The Negro Resurrectionist
The Grade-School Chum

(Rest)

The Negro Resurrectionist
Uh uhnn.

The Grade-School Chum
Then its thuh slammer, Stupid.
I gotcha by thuh throat, admit it.

The Negro Resurrectionist
The Grade-School Chum
The Negro Resurrectionist
The Grade-School Chum

(Rest)

The Negro Resurrectionist
Ok.
I mean, whatever.
Yr uh bastards bastard.
But fine. Alright, I guess.
I mean, who is she to me?

The Grade-School Chum
The Negro Resurrectionist

The Grade-School Chum
Theres a good boy. Heh-Heh-Heh.
Heres a little in advance.

> The Grade-School Chum tosses him a single gold coin.
> He takes the coin but feels like shit.

Scene 4: "For the Love of the Venus" (conclusion)

The Baron Docteur watches from one place, The Venus from another.
The Bride-to-Be, masquerading as a Hottentot Venus, and
The Young Man stare at each other.

The Hottentot Venus
The Young Man
The Hottentot Venus
The Young Man

(Rest)

The Young Man
Tell her Im smitten.

The Uncle
I think she knows.

The Young Man
By these knees Im bending on
True Venus
Im forever thine.
I'll never change.
Promise me the same.
Uncle, put that on yr tongue then in her tongue then in her ear.
(Rest)
What is her answer?

The Uncle
She promises constancy but
as we lose uh skin layer every day
so will she shrug her old self off.

The Young Man
Shrug all you want but keep thuh core.
(Rest)
Answer.

> She removes her disguise and again
> becomes The Bride-to-Be.

The Bride-to-Be
Dearheart: Your true love stands before you.

> He gives her a red heart box of chocolates.
> Love Tableau.
> Curtain.
> The Baron Docteur applauds.

Scene 3: A Brief History of Chocolate

The planets align.

The Venus
(Rest)
A BRIEF HISTORY OF CHOCOLATE:
It is written in the ancient chronicles
that the Gods one day looked down with pity
pity on the people as they struggled.
The Gods resolved to visit the people
and teach them the ways of Love
for Love helps in times of hardship.
As an act of Love one God gives to the people
a little shrub that had, until then, belonged
only to the Gods.
This was the cacao tree.
(Rest)
Time passed.
Time passed uhgain:
We find ourselves in the 19th century.
The Aztec word *cacao* literally "food of the Gods"
becomes *chocolate* and *cocoa*.
The *cacao* bean, once used as money
becomes an exotic beverage.
The Spanish were known to die for their chocolate.
In the New World, they were also known to kill for it.
In Europe the church wages a campaign against chocolate
on the grounds that it was tainted by the character
of its heathen inventors.
"Chocolate is the damnable agent of necromancers and
    sorcerers,"

said one French cleric circa 1620.
The Pilgrims in America. Some said they fled England
    because of chocolate.
But thats another story.
(Rest)
Chocolate was soon mixed with milk and sugar
and formed into lozenges which one could eat on the run.
Chocolate lozenges are now found in a variety of shapes
mixed with everything from nuts to brandy.
Chocolate is a recognized emotional stimulant,
for doctors have recently noticed the tendency of some
    persons,
especially women,
to go on chocolate binges
binges either *after* emotionally upsetting incidents
or in an effort to allow themselves *to handle* an incident
which may be emotionally upsetting.
This information is interesting in that it has become the
    practice
to present a gift of chocolates when professing Love.
This practice, begun some time ago, continues to this day.
(Rest)
While chocolate was once used as a stimulant and source of
    nutrition
it is primarily today a great source of fat,
and, of course, pleasure.
(Rest)

Scene 2: The Venus Hottentot Tells the Story of Her Life

The Negro Resurrectionist fingers his new gold coin.

The Venus
Whered ya get that?

The Negro Resurrectionist
I found it.
Just this morning on the street.

The Venus
Yr lucky.

The Negro Resurrectionist
Im not lying!!

The Venus
I didnt say you were.

The Venus
The Negro Resurrectionist
The Venus
The Negro Resurrectionist

(Rest)

The Venus
How long you lived here?

The Negro Resurrectionist
Me? Ive lived in this town all my life.

I used to dig up people
dead ones. You know,
after theyd been buried.
Doctors pay a lot for corpses
but "Resurrection" is illegal
and I was always this close to getting arrested.
This Jail-Watchmans jobs much more carefree.

The Venus
You dont have anything you miss?
Yr lucky, Watchman.
I always dream of home
in every spare minute.
It was a shitty shitty life but oh I miss it.
Whats that sound outside, crowds?

The Negro Resurrectionist
Yes.
Yr still a star.

The Venus
Dont let them in.

The Negro Resurrectionist
Dont worry.

The Venus
The Negro Resurrectionist
The Venus
The Negro Resurrectionist

(Rest)

The Venus
Whats that outside?
Crowds?

The Negro Resurrectionist
Just rain.
We're having lousy weather.
Its just rain.

The Venus
I was born near the coast, Watchman.
Journeyed some worked some
ended up here.
I would live here I thought but only for uh minute!
Make a mint.
Had plans to.
He had a beard.
Big bags of money!
Where wuz I?
Fell in love. Hhh.
Tried my hand at French.
Gave me a haircut
and thuh claps.
You get thuh picture, huh?
Dont look at me
dont look . . .
(Rest)

She dies.

The Negro Resurrectionist
(Rest)
"Early in the 19th century a poor wretched woman was exhibited in England under the appellation of *The Hottentot Venus*. With an intensely ugly figure, distorted beyond all European notions of beauty, she was said to possess precisely the kind of shape which is most admired among her countrymen, the Hottentots."

The year was 1810, three years after the Bill for the Abolition of the Slave-Trade had been passed in Parliament, and among protests and denials, horror and fascination her show went on. She died in Paris 5 years later: A plaster cast of her body was once displayed, along with her skeleton, in the *Musee de l'Homme*.
(Rest)

Scene 1: Final Chorus

The Negro Resurrectionist
I regret to inform you that thuh Venus Hottentot iz dead.

All
Dead!

The Negro Resurrectionist
There wont be inny show tuhnite.

The Venus
Miss me Miss me Miss me

The Grade-School Chum
Exposure iz what killed her
nothin on in our cold weather.

The Negro Resurrectionist
23 days in uh row it rained.

The Baron Docteur
I say she died of drink.

The Negro Resurrectionist
It was the cold I think.

The Venus
Hear ye hear ye hear ye
thuh Venus Hottentot iz dead.
There wont be inny show tuhnite.

The Grade-School Chum

I know yr dissuhpointed.
I hate tuh let you down.

All

Gimmie gimmie back my buck!

The Venus

I come from miles and miles and miles and miles

All

Hotsey-Totsey!

The Negro Resurrectionist

Diggidy-diggidy-diggidy-diggidy.

All

Diggidy-diggidy-diggidy-dawg.

The Chorus of the 8 Human Wonders

Turn uhway
dont look
cover yr face
cover yr eyes.

All

Drum Drum Drum Drum.
Hur-ry Hur-ry Step in Step in.
(Rest)
Thuh Venus Hottentot iz dead.

The Venus

Tail end of the tale for there must be uh end
is that Venus, Black Goddess, was shameless, she sinned or else
completely unknowing thuh Godfearin ways, she stood
showing her ass off in her iron cage.
When Death met Love Death deathd Love
and left Love tuh rot
au naturel end for thuh Miss Hottentot.
Loves soul, which was tidy, hides in heaven, yes, thats it
Loves corpse stands on show in museum. Please
visit.

All
Diggidy-diggidy-diggidy
Diggidy-diggidy-diggidy-dawg!

The Negro Resurrectionist
A Scene of Love:

The Venus
Kiss me *Kiss* me *Kiss* me *Kiss*

End of Play

A Glossary of Medical Terms

Annular ligament—a large muscle in the wrist
Atlas—the part of the spine that supports the head
Attolens and **Attrahens Aurem**—the muscles of the ear
Avoirdupois—personal weight
Axilla—the armpit
Calvarium—the skull lacking the lower jaw
Cervicalis ascendens—a neck muscle near the upper ribs
Clavicle—the collar bone
Coccyx—the tail bone
Conjunctiva—mucous membrane lining the eyeball
Dorso-epitrochlear muscle—a muscle similar to the **Latissimus dorsi** found in nonhuman animals
Dorsum—the back surface of an area
Extensor communis digitorum—a muscle of the forearm
Extensor minimi digiti—a slender muscle running through the arm and into the hand
Extensor primi internodii pollicis—the smallest muscle of the arm
Fascia—a sheet of connective tissue
Femur—the thigh bone (the longest, largest and strongest bone in the skeleton)
Flexor brevis digitorum pedis—a muscle in the middle of the sole of the foot
Formal cartilage's tip—a.k.a. the xyphoid process, the cartilage at the tip of the breastbone
Fundus—part of the aperture of an organ
Gluteus maximus—the muscle of the buttocks
Gluteus medius—the muscle on the outer surface of the pelvis covered by **Gluteus maximus**
Humeral bone—the upper arm bone

Labia majora—the outer vaginal lips

Labia minora—the inner vaginal lips

Latissimus dorsi muscle—a large flat muscle covering the lumbar and lower half of the dorsal region

Levator anguli scapulae—a muscle at the back and side of the neck

Levator claviculae—a muscle of the clavicle area first noted by Dr. McWhinnie

Malar—two small bones forming the prominence of the cheek

Mammae—the breasts

Mastoid process—the bone behind the ear, part of the jaw

Metacarpo-phalangeal—the hand and finger bones

Nymphae—the inner lips of the vulva

Occipitalis muscle—the muscle at the back of the skull

Omo-hyoid—a muscle of the neck, passing across the side of the neck

Os calcis—the heel bone

Patella—the knee bone

Pelvis at crest of Ilium—the top crest of the hip bone

Perineum—the muscle between genitals and anus

Prepuce—the folds of skin enveloping the clitoris

Pubes—the pubic region

Pudendum—external genital organs, especially of a woman

Radius— the arm bone on the thumb side

Sacro-lumbalis muscle—located in the external portion of the erector (lower) spine

Scapula—the bone comprising the back part of the shoulder

Septum—the inner wall of the nose separating the nostrils

Septum narium/nares—the inner nasal area

Serratus magnus—a muscle in the chest

Splenius colli—a muscle at the back of the neck

Steatopygia—an excessive developement of fat on the buttocks especially of females, which is common among the so-called Hottentots and some Negro peoples

Sterno-mastoid—a large muscle passing downwards along the front of the neck

Sternum—the breastbone

Teres minor—the narrow muscle of the shoulder area

Thorax—the chest cavity

Tibia—the leg bone between the knee and ankle

Trachelo-mastoid—a muscle running from the jaw area around to the back

Tragus—the prominence at the front of the opening of the ear
Transverse process—a muscular-like lever which serves as the attachment of muscles which move the different parts of the spine
Trapezius—a muscle covering the upper and back part of the neck and shoulders
Triceps—muscles situated on the back of the arm
Trochanters—the upper part of the thigh bone
Tubercle—the protuberance near the head of the rib
Ulna—the arm bone on the little finger side
Umbilicus—the belly button
Vertex—the top of the head

A Glossary of Chocolates

Bouchon Fraise—cupcake-shaped, either dark chocolate or buttercream, filled with either strawberry crème fraîche or cognac flavor, respectively
Capezzoli di Venere—"the nipples of Venus," breast-shaped mounds in dark or light chocolate with a red or white iced "nipple" on top; crème fraîche often inside
Enfant de Bruxelles—dark chocolate lozenge with an image of a little African child stamped upon it; coffee and chocolate crème fraîche inside
Escargot Lait—fashioned in the shape of a snail's shell; milk chocolate with praliné inside
Petits coeurs—"little hearts" of solid chocolate
Pharaon—a solid lozenge, either dark or buttercream, with the image of a pharaoh's head stamped upon it
Rhum Caramel—cube-shaped, dark chocolate with light caramel; crème fraîche and rum flavor inside

About Suzan-Lori Parks

My family moved around a lot which, so I'm told, if you've got the inclination, can make a writer out of you. I started writing as a kid, kept at it, some people encouraged me others didn't, and here I am today. The ones who encouraged me are pleased as punch, the ones who didn't I don't know what they think because I don't speak with them much these days.

I first heard about the woman called the Hottentot Venus at a cocktail party. Liz Diamond was talking about her and I was eavesdropping. As I listened bells started going off in my head and I knew this Saartjie Baartman woman was going to end up in a play of mine. She was a woman with a remarkable bottom, a woman with a past, and that got me interested in her.

"Tell all the Truth but tell it slant," as Emily Dickinson says. With *Venus* my angle is this: *History, Memory, Dis-Memory, Remembering, Dismembering, Love, Distance, Time, a Show.*

Most of my other plays are included in *The America Play and Other Works* (TCG); I've written some radio plays and some screenplays including *Girl 6* which premiered in 1996 and was directed by Spike Lee. I'm a graduate of Mount Holyoke College, where I studied writing with James Baldwin. I'm a member of New Dramatists and have been awarded the Whiting Award, the Cal Arts/Herb Alpert Award, 2 Obie awards for my plays (*Venus* was one of them), a grant from the Kennedy Center New American Plays Fund, 2 grants from the National Endowment for the Arts, and others. I've taught playwriting at schools all over the place including the Yale School of Drama.

Right now I'm working on a tv pilot, another screenplay, the 2nd draft of my first novel and 3 new plays.